# HISTORY OF CANADA

NOTES

COLES EDITORIAL BOARD

COLES notes

ISBN 0-7740-3442-4

© COPYRIGHT 1988 AND PUBLISHED BY
**COLES PUBLISHING COMPANY LIMITED**
TORONTO—CANADA
PRINTED IN CANADA

Manufactured by Webcom Limited
Cover finish: Webcom's Exclusive **Duracoat**

# CONTENTS

I. To The Constitutional Act of 1791 .............. 1
II. Economic Development of Canada, 1791-1812 ....................................... 8
III. The War of 1812 .............................. 9
IV. The Expansion of Canada, 1814-1837 .......... 11
V. The 1837 Rebellion in Canada ................. 13
VI. Durham's Report ............................ 19
VII. The Arrival of Responsible Government in Canada ..................................... 22
VIII. Canada, 1849 to Confederation ............... 25
IX. The Confederation of Canada, 1867 ........... 27
X. The Canadian Constitution — A Summary ................................. 33
XI. Macdonald's Administration, 1867-1873 ...................................... 37
XII. The Liberal Administration, 1873-1878 ......... 41
XIII. The Conservatives in Power, 1878-1896 ........ 43
XIV. The Laurier Ministry, 1896-1911 ............... 49
XV. The Conservative Administration, 1911-1917 ..................................... 57
XVI. The Union Government, 1917-1921 ............ 60
XVII. King's Liberals in Power, 1921-1930 ............ 64
XVIII. Bennett's Conservatives in Power, 1930-1935 ..................................... 69
XIX. King's Liberals Return to Power, 1935-1945 ..................................... 72
XX. The Liberals Retain Power, 1945-1957 .......... 77
XXI. Diefenbaker's Conservatives in Power, 1957-1963 ..................................... 85
XXII. Pearson's Liberals Rule as a Minority, 1963-1968 ..................................... 89
XXIII. Trudeau in Power, 1968-1979 ................. 91
XXIV. The Turbulent Years, 1979-1985 ............... 102
Bibliography..................................... 107

# HISTORY OF CANADA
# I. To The Constitutional Act of 1791

## 1. Early History

The history of Canada really begins as much as 35,000 years ago when, it is thought, roving bands of hunters arrived in North America. But, because no written records exist for these early societies, the period up to the arrival of Europeans is termed "prehistory." Much work has been done in the past few years on Canadian prehistory, and only a start has been made in uncovering the early story of Canada.

The ancient people hunted big game including, it seems possible, mammoth and mastodon. As the glaciers of the ice age retreated from Canada, these peoples moved east and south and their societies changed. At least one site in eastern Canada has been dated at approximately 7000 B.C. New sites are being constantly uncovered throughout Canada.

When Europeans arrived, the variety of peoples and cultures they found was quite astonishing. Every band of hunters, it seemed, had beliefs and practices that were, at least in some details, distinct from all the others.

Broad groups can be identified as follows:

1. Hunters who migrated from place to place, living on the various food sources in the forests and along the coastlines. These groups included people as diverse as the Micmacs of the Maritimes, the Ojibway of northern Ontario, and the Athabascans of the Mackenzie River valley.

2. Bison hunters of the plains, including the Cree and Blackfoot.

3. Village dwellers and fishermen of the B.C. coast, with a great range of cultures and languages, including the Nootka, Kwakiutl, and others.

4. The Inuit of the far north, living on caribou and sea mammals, and including such groups as the Mackenzie Eskimo, and the Copper Eskimo.

5. Village dwellers, traders, and corn growers of the lower Great Lakes, of which the Huron were the most prominent.

These people developed tools for survival that were vital to the success of the later Europeans. These devices included the canoe, the snowshoe, snow-goggles, and pemmican. Without the lessons taught by Canadian natives, European settlers could not have survived. This was especially so in Canada, where European colonists depended, for well over a century, on the wealth brought in by the fur trade, and hence, by their native allies.

1

## 2. New France

Quebec was the first permanent European settlement in Canada. It was founded by Champlain in 1608. (Shortly before, Sir Humphrey Gilbert had failed to establish English settlements in Newfoundland. St. John's, however, dates its founding two years after the founding of Quebec. It now appears that there was at least one Viking settlement in Newfoundland before the 11th century.)

Quebec was a fur trading depot, and Champlain spent much of his time cementing alliances with the surrounding native peoples. The most important of these were the Huron, who lived in villages and depended on corn growing and trade to support themselves. Since the common enemy of all these people was the Iroquois, Champlain agreed to go to war against the Iroquois. He also sent missionaries, most notably the Jesuits, to the Huron villages to hold this alliance. In return, the Hurons and other natives brought their furs to Quebec.

At first, Quebec was really the property of a fur trading company, and there were very few Frenchmen living there. Even so, it was a French colony, and became France's most important center in North America. The company, not France, brought out the early settlers. These arrived in a trickle. The missionary efforts of the Jesuits were responsible for many converts in the early days, and when Fort Ste. Marie was established among the Hurons, near modern-day Midland, Ontario, there were almost as many Frenchmen there as there were in Quebec. Small settlements also arose around the fur posts in present-day Nova Scotia, and these also depended on the fur trade.

But Quebec was the key to the French colony, and the Hurons were the key to Quebec's success. In 1649-50, the Iroquois, armed with guns sold to them by the Dutch of New Amsterdam, destroyed the Hurons, drove out the Jesuits, and almost destroyed New France.

Small settlements along the St. Lawrence had been added at Trois Rivières, and Ville Marie (Montreal), but there were still less than 3,000 French settlers in Canada at this time. They could not have held off the Iroquois, especially as the Hurons, a much more numerous people, had been destroyed in battles.

Louis XIV had recently come to power in France and he was determined to make New France a strong colony. He sent out Talon, a regiment of soldiers and, later, Frontenac, to strengthen the colony. Military expeditions, and diplomatic talks helped to establish a precarious peace with the Iroquois.

In 1663, King Louis brought the colony under the complete authority of the throne. The local government was reorganized under a tribunal of the governor, the bishop, and the intendant. The first intendant was Jean Talon, whose program was to expand the colony and vitalize its economy. Laval, the bishop, was just as determined to make religious authority the dominant power in the colony, and he relied on the Jesuits for help in his program. Frontenac, an old soldier and nobleman with many debts, became governor somewhat later, and undertook to make the governor's office the most powerful in New France. The result was that no one was dominant, and a constant struggle for power between intendant, bishop and governor began. This system was to plague New France to the end.

French traders — *coureurs de bois* — went into the interior of the continent to replace the scattered Huron, and to bring furs direct to Quebec. They learned native languages, often married native women, and created a fusion of native and European society not seen in the growing English colonies to the south. Louis Joliet, a trader, journeyed down the Mississippi with Marquette, a Jesuit missionary, and added a vast area to France's claim to territory in North America. La Salle completed this exploration, and established a fur post on the Mississippi that survived his own failures, and became a permanent French base in the heart of the continent.

After 1663, only the French and English remained as important colonizing powers in North America. The English had forced the Dutch out of New Amsterdam, and had thus become the major Iroquois ally. In 1670, with the help of the French traders Radisson and Groseilliers, the English also established themselves on Hudson Bay. This spurred the fur traders of Quebec to drive deeper into North America in the search for furs. A struggle for the control of a vast area of the continent was set in motion. By the 1730's La Vérendrye and his sons had penetrated as far west as the Black Hills of Dakota.

This struggle went ahead even while England and France were at peace. After Talon returned to France, Louis XIV lost much of his interest in Canada. As the years went by, France returned to its general neglect of Canada. England took much the same view of its colonies. Although settlers from England and other parts of Europe swelled the population of the English settlements, New France did not enjoy a similar immigration.

New France had internal problems that were mostly the product of the fur trade, the backbone of the colony's economy. And yet these problems would have been less severe if there had been more colonists on the St. Lawrence.

The trade required that young, active men leave Quebec for long periods. This left a manpower shortage that was reflected in the slow progress of agricultural settlement. And yet, the authorities could not afford to be too strict with these young men, for if they were not out in the woods trading with the Indians, the furs would not come in. If the furs didn't arrive, they could not be sold to Europe, and the whole economy of the colony would collapse. As time went on, and the traders travelled farther and farther inland in pursuit of furs, this problem became worse. Scattered settlements did arise around fur posts at

Cataraqui (Kingston), Detroit, Michilimacinac (between Lakes Huron and Michigan), and down the Mississippi, but these were small supply posts of a few men far outnumbered by the Indian bands surrounding them. The major French settlement was concentrated on the St. Lawrence.

This community of the St. Lawrence centred around the habitant who cultivated his land, paid the dues demanded by the seigneur, and raised his many children in an atmosphere that was much freer than that in France. The growth of the colony was based on the large families of the habitant, for after the return of Talon few new settlers came from France.

The habitant had been given his land by the seigneur, a nobleman who had been granted a large tract of land in the name of the king. The seigneur was required to bring in settlers, divide his lands among them, provide a mill and other facilities, and received, in turn, rents and other dues from the habitants. As the system grew, these seigneurs provided local leadership in peace and war, and were fairly close to the habitants because they never grew rich enough to become grand noblemen.

The colony was a lively frontier community, and the fur trade provided much of the excitement. Brandy was the source of much quarrelling and division among the authorities. The Jesuit missionaries condemned the effects of the sale of brandy to the Indians. They complained that the fur traders were undermining the morals of young Indian women by their unchristian conduct, and of Indian warriors by their sale of brandy. Their complaints came back to the bishop, who complained in turn to the governor. This latter official agreed, until attacks on brandy began to undermine the fur trade. Then he took up the cause of the fur traders, who accused the Jesuits of harming the best interests of the colony. The result was a running quarrel between the religious authorities and the supporters of the governor.

## 3. The Struggle for North America

The fur trade also involved the French in running competition with the growing English colonies. Agricultural settlement pushes out fur-bearing animals. To protect their economy, the French felt they had to hold the English colonists east of the Appalachians. As this aim coincided with the desire of the Indians to hold their lands against the advance of European colonists, the French and various Indian groups were often in alliance. This, in turn, aligned both groups against the English frontiersmen. The result was a series of clashes in the forests of North America, and a growing demand from the English colonies that England conquer New France. Sometimes these colonists took matters into their own hands, especially when they could use their growing fleet of ships. This put the French settlements along the Atlantic coast in

Acadia on the front line. After the French government built Louisbourg, an armed fortress, the sea attacks were concentrated on that point.

In land warfare, the French in both Quebec and Acadia adopted the guerilla warfare of their Indian allies. They raided English settlements in surprise attacks that were completed long before the militia could gather to defend the settlement. In New France, along the St. Lawrence, farmhouses were built close together in a long string of settlements that was useful in case the English attacked by land. The great stretches of forest between New France and the English colonies were also a major line of defense, and made it possible for a small colony such as New France to hold off much larger land forces. The major weakness in this line of defense was the sea. But a full-scale war by sea would involve the navies of both England and France, and this meant that the fate of New France would be decided in Europe.

As the eighteenth century advanced, England and France became involved in a competition for colonies. This rivalry, carried on in India, North America, and elsewhere, was an extension of the European wars involving both powers. It was aggravated by the restrictive trading terms of rival navigation laws, which meant that any area of the world controlled by one power was automatically closed to the trade of the other. This meant that the winner would be the power that gained a greater number of strategic colonies.

War between the two powers flared up throughout the century. The first of the series broke out over a dispute involving the throne of Spain. Louis XIV wanted one of his relatives to become King of Spain, but other European powers, including England, did not want him to gain control of Spain. At the end of the War of the Spanish Succession, the Treaty of Utrecht (1713) confirmed England as the paramount sea power and handed Acadia (Nova Scotia) over to her. At the same time, France waived claims to Newfoundland and Hudson Bay.

After the war of the Austrian Succession, the Treaty of Aix-la-Chapelle (1748) returned the fortress of Louisbourg to France, from whom it had been captured during the war. This treaty was really more of a truce; in fact, in North America some form of Anglo-French warfare persisted until the next formal European outbreak.

This came in the form of the Seven Years' War (1756-63). In 1755, the British had removed the French-speaking population from Nova Scotia, on the grounds that they had refused to take the oath of allegiance to fight against France should the need arise. These people were re-settled throughout British colonies.

The Seven Years' War resulted in French defeat and confirmation of England as the colonizing power in North America (and India). British naval supremacy had both prevented French reinforcement and allowed penetration of the French colonial waterways for such expeditions as the capture of Louisbourg (1758) and Quebec (1759). French Canada really came to an end with the fall of Montreal in 1760. The Treaty of Paris (1763) installed England as owner of all North America east of the Mississippi.

## 4. The Settlement

The French colony in Canada was not large by modern standards. In 1763 there were only 80,000 French settlers in all North America. This is roughly the present population of Verdun, Quebec.

The English design for Quebec within the Empire was contained in the Quebec Act of 1774. This was a reasonably successful attempt to conciliate the French Canadians. At the same time, it acted as one of the contributing causes of most of the other English colonies leaving the Empire in the American Revolution (1776-1783).

The Quebec Act recognized the Catholic Church (which antagonized the Protestant colonies to the south). It also laid down a constitution which did not allow a legislative assembly (which the older colonies took to be a threat to their own assemblies). Further, it set the boundary of Quebec to include the Ohio River valley (which made permanent the temporary boundary of 1763 and prevented any expansion of the older American colonies to the east of the valley).

The Act also confirmed the right of the Catholic Church to collect tithes from the people of that faith. French law in such civil areas as semi-feudal (seigneurial) rights and dues, matrimony and land tenure was retained. The seat of power lay with an appointed governor and a non-elected advisory council with English and French, Catholic and Protestant members.

The Act was a clear effort to ensure the loyalty of the upperclass and trading French community, together with the church establishment. The fur trade was protected by the prevention of competition in the Ohio valley and upper Mississippi from the Albany and New York market. This provision cancelled out the merchants' opposition to a non-elected government.

During the American Revolution, the church and the landed classes were benevolently neutral, if not enthusiastically loyal to England. The lower classes were interested neither in fighting for nor against established authority.

As a community, the French Canadians realized that they would still be a minority in any new American organization, and preferred the shelter of the Quebec Act and the preferred markets in Europe which would be open to a British colony, whoever won the Revolution.

In 1775, an expedition from the revolutionary colonies captured Montreal, but was unable to take Quebec, and so failed. In 1776, the Royal Navy took command of the St. Lawrence, never to lose it during the war.

The Treaty of Versailles (1783) ended the American Revolution and recognized the U.S.A., and new boundaries were set out for Canada. In the Great Lakes area, the lakes themselves became the southern boundary, thus removing the Ohio valley from Canada and the Montreal fur trade area. This tended to force Canadian trappers to work across the country to the west and north of the lakes.

Another crucial result of the American Revolution was the loyalist migration. About one in three of the people in the colonies had been opposed to the revolution, and about 100,000 decided to migrate at the end of the war. They were partly driven to this by the American refusal to honor the non-discriminatory terms of the peace treaty.

The loyalists represented a wide stratum of the colonial population and all had the common experience of losing most or all of their material possessions. Of the 40,000 who came to Canada, about three-quarters came to Nova Scotia and the rest to Quebec.

The situation in the Maritimes was handled by the creation in 1784 of a new colony, New Brunswick. This was composed mainly of the new immigrants on the line north of the Bay of Fundy. The rest attached themselves to the established community around Halifax, Nova Scotia. Loyalists outnumbered earlier settlers in these two colonies by about two to one.

The migration into Quebec of 10,000 loyalists also caused radical administrative change. With their background of English land tenure and common law, they were entirely unwilling to accept the seigneurial land tenure and French legal system so recently confirmed in the colony. In particular, they were unwilling to accept a non-elected system of government.

As a result, in 1791, the British parliament passed the Constitutional Act which solved most of the problems of the new situation. The old colony of Quebec was split, the eastern section being largely French Canadian and known as Lower Canada, the western and formerly almost entirely uninhabited section being largely immigrant loyalist and English. It should not be assumed that Upper Canada, as this loyalist section was known, was created by splitting an existing populated French Canadian colony.

Lower Canada retained its confirmed French institutions of the 1774 Quebec Act, namely, seigneurial land tenure, the Catholic church and French civil law. French Canadians and Catholics were in the preponderant majority. They received, however, a definite constitutional improvement in the granting of an elected assembly, largely in response to the demands of the English element, especially traders, in the colony.

Upper Canada, of course, received English institutions, laws, and an elected assembly. The whole administrative reorganization of French Canada as a result of the American Revolution meant that there were now four English colonies created out of what had been enemy territory in 1760, whereas the original British territory on the continent had largely been lost as a result of that revolution.

## II. Economic Development of Canada, 1791-1812

The Canadian colonies developed individually after 1791. Immigrants tended to favor the Maritimes. At the end of the period, the total population of the Maritimes was about 100,000. Most of the labor force was involved in either fishing or lumbering.

The problem of the Maritimes was competition from the U.S.A. This, despite the continued protection of the (British) Navigation Acts, which gave Empire producers complete preference within Empire markets, both for produce and its transport. The other colonies founded their economic prosperity on these acts, and their economy grew in the protected Empire market. An additional source of economic expansion was the outbreak of the French Revolution and Napoleonic Wars. The development of the blockade system in the latter forced Britain to look to British North America not only for produce, but for ships to carry out the blockade. Shipbuilding was the basis for considerable prosperity in the Maritimes.

Rapid population growth accompanied the economic expansion outside the Maritimes. In Lower Canada, this was largely the result of natural increase (i.e., surplus of births over deaths). This contributed to a threefold expansion in the two decades under review. The main center in Lower Canada was Montreal. This mercantile center depended extensively on the fur trade, which was largely in the hands of the English element. As a result, the economy was mainly outside the control of the French Canadians.

In the same twenty years, Upper Canada's population increased over five-fold, to some 90,000. This, however, was mostly caused by immigration largely from the U.S.A. The principal governor of the time was John Graves Simcoe, whose main program was to produce in North America as exact a copy as possible of British life and institutions.

The main activity in Upper Canada took place around York (now Toronto) on Lake Ontario. This center had been chosen as the colonial capital in 1793. The main population movement was into the central southern section of the colony, although Kingston remained the largest single center until after 1820.

In Upper Canada, roads were constructed both to open up the new territory and to allow the easy movement of British troops. The land itself was distributed on a reasonably generous scale, the main requirement from the settler being the oath of loyalty to the British Crown.

In all the colonies, the main emphasis was on the pioneering and economic aspects of life; socially and culturally, British North America was immature and semi-barren.

## III. The War of 1812

### 1. Causes

a. The Treaty of Versailles (1783) had not really solved many of the differences between the British and the U.S.A.; particularly, the fur trade, British occupancy of the northwestern forts, and British relations with Indians in territory surrendered to the United States had caused friction on the continent.

b. Jay's Treaty (1794) had only partly settled these difficulties, and had expired in 1804.

c. A vociferous group of expansionists had recently been elected to Congress. They were committed to the concept that it was the "manifest destiny" of the U.S.A. to control the whole of North America and advocated the use of force to this end. They were known as the "Warhawks", and included such people as Henry Clay and John Calhoun.

d. U.S. settlers in the western frontier areas were convinced that British fur traders were encouraging the Indians, and their leader, Tecumseh, to engage in hostilities against the frontiersmen. In particular, they resented the trading of guns and ammunition for furs.

e. There was extreme annoyance in the U.S. over the British insistence on the right of maritime search of any ships approaching Europe. Macon's Act, which was passed after the lapsing of Jay's Treaty, declared that the U.S.A. would go to war on the side of either Britain or France, depending on which country ceased restricting U.S. shipping in European waters. Napoleon succeeded in convincing the U.S.A. (wrongly) that he intended to accommodate them in this matter, and war was declared on Britain.

As a matter of fact, Britain had withdrawn the offending orders-in-council, under which U.S. shipping was stopped and searched, a few days before the declaration of war. Trans-Atlantic communications at that time took some six weeks each way, so that the war was under way and hostile acts committed before the news of the withdrawal became known in the U.S.A.

### 2. Course

a. The land battles took place entirely in North America. All the important battles, except the Battle of New Orleans, were fought over a wide-spread area of Upper Canada.

At first, there was a great deal of local apathy and an acceptance of inevitable defeat. The British commander, Brock, crossed into the U.S.A. in the Lake St. Clair area, capturing Detroit. He then returned to the Niagara area, where he was killed in the defeat of a U.S. invasion force at Queenston Heights. Brock's vigor and sacrifice rallied the colony and confidence returned to the settlers.

In 1813, the U.S. forces, mainly militia, pushed into Upper Canada across the Niagara frontier as far as Stoney Creek. They rapidly took control of the western end of Lake Ontario, capturing and reducing the capital at York. In 1814, this force was fought to a draw at Lundy's Lane and driven back into the U.S.A.

In Lower Canada, the French Canadian militia remained loyal and in 1812 it held off a U.S. attack on Montreal. In the following year, it defeated the U.S. forces at Chateauguay and Crysler's Farm.

The collapse of Napoleon in Europe in 1814 enabled the British to send veteran troops from the Peninsula. These completely outmatched the U.S. militia, and in the same year an invading British force easily penetrated to Washington, where public buildings were burned in revenge for the earlier burning of York.

The war then came to a ragged conclusion. Although there was a British defeat at New Orleans in 1814, in actual fact it was after the two governments had agreed to suspend hostilities.

b. At sea, the new U.S. naval forces were, surprisingly, often more than a match for the Royal Navy. The war consisted mainly of separate engagements on the lakes and off the eastern seaboard. The numbers of ships involved were not large; in some cases, the battles consisted of duels between single ships. Most U.S. ships were privateers fitted out for the war. Some Maritimers became wealthy operating privateers which preyed on American shipping.

## 3. Results

a. The war showed that there was a definite intention in British North America not to become part of the U.S.A. This was true of both English and French Canada, and the war served as a needed tie based on resistance to Americanism.

b. Peace was agreed to by the Treaty of Ghent (1814).

**Terms**
1. The pre-war boundaries were confirmed.
2. Outstanding problems between Britain and the U.S.A. were to be settled by a number of joint committees set up under the treaty.

**Results**
1. The treaty inaugurated the settlement of Anglo-American problems by negotiation, a practice never later departed from.
2. The resulting Rush-Bagot Treaty (1817) reduced naval forces on the Great Lakes to the absolute minimum needed for law enforcement.
3. A convention in 1818 established the 49th parallel as the boundary between Canada and the U.S.A., from the Lake of the Woods to the Rocky Mountains.
4. At the same time, eastern maritime fishing difficulties were temporarily settled by allowing U.S. fishing vessels to enter Canadian ports for supplies, but prohibiting them from fishing within three miles of the shore.

## IV. The Expansion of Canada, 1814-1837

### 1. The Northwest

In 1789, Alexander Mackenzie had discovered the great river to be named after him, and in 1793 he reached the Pacific. The fur trade moved westwards in his footsteps. In this expansion the Hudson's Bay Company had the advantage of better organization and more capital.

The Montreal fur traders, as a result, decided to end internal competition by combining to form the Northwestern Company. Friction between the two organizations followed, and often turned into open hostilities.

In 1812, Lork Selkirk, of the Hudson's Bay Company, formed a settlement of Scots colonists in the Red River valley near what is now Winnipeg. In 1816, the Northwest Company prevailed upon the half-breeds in the area to attack the colony, after which the area fell under the control of the Montreal group.

In 1821, however, both companies ended their competition and merged. On the surface, the Northwest Company received a reasonable settlement out of the merger, but in fact the Hudson's Bay Company had emerged the victor in the struggle.

### 2. The Economy, from the Treaty of Ghent to The Rebellion of 1837

After the end of the Napoleonic Wars (1815), the fur trade entered a long decline. The colonies became more solidly committed to an agricultural economy. This was encouraged by the system of land grants, by which large tracts were given to individuals and organizations for development.

One of the latter was the Canada Land Company (1826), which operated in south central Ontario and brought out immigrants, at the same time providing local amenities for them.

There were, however, difficulties. In Lower Canada, the larger seigneuries had tended to pass to speculators, and new settlers lacked the capital to buy the better areas from them. In Upper Canada, the land grant policy became erratic. Although men who had served in the War of 1812, and loyalists, had no difficulty in obtaining land, more recent settlers were kept off the better concessions. In Upper Canada, also, areas had been allocated by the Constitutional Act of 1791 for the benefit of the Protestant Church (the Clergy Reserves) and these were allowed to remain undeveloped. There was also a land speculation problem in this colony.

By the time of the rebellion of 1837, the population of Upper Canada had grown to almost 400,000, but there were occasional economic depressions which held back expansion. There was already, at this time, some difference in approach towards progress, apparent or real, north and south of the border, so that the less conservative immigrant tended to head for the U.S.A. rather than British North America.

The mainspring of the Canadian economy throughout the period was Montreal. It was the center of the natural transport complex based on the Great Lakes, while remaining the cheapest gateway to Europe for movement of goods from the expanding frontier. It seemed entirely possible that the city would become the financial and economic capital of the entire sub-continent.

However, in 1825 the Erie Canal was completed. This linked the all-weather port of New York with Buffalo, and thence the entire frontier in the northwest. The Welland Canal, which by-passed the Niagara Rapids and Falls, was a partial answer to this development. State financial aid had been necessary for its construction, and on opening (1829) it became state property.

Another problem was that the industrial revolution was in full swing in Britain, and with it the demand for laissez-faire economic policies by the merchant class. In the U.S.A., however, the eastern manufacturers were demanding a protective tariff against British imports. It followed that Montreal importers would not be able to sell in the U.S., while exporters to Britain would not be able to compete in the home islands. The milling industry was particularly prone to loss, for U.S. wheat milled in Canada entered Britain as empire produce.

A third problem for the Montreal traders was that they found themselves increasingly an English minority in a French Canadian community. Further, this community, whose members had been generally excluded from the merchant class, did not share the same economic expansionist aims as the Montreal mercantile interests.

# V. The 1837 Rebellion in Canada

## 1. Causes
### a. Common to Upper and Lower Canada
#### i. Political

The 1791 Constitutional Act had not proved to be satisfactory. It had been established when the feeling in Britain was that the American colonies had been lost because there had been too much democratic control. The intention of the Act was to prevent the same mistake in the rest of British North America.

The Act had stipulated that a governor, sent out from Britain, should rule with an appointed executive council to advise him. In addition, there was an appointed legislative council (roughly parallel to the British House of Lords) and an elected legislative assembly (roughly, the Commons). Generally, the governor's advisors in the executive council tended to be also members of the appointed legislative council. A further preventive of popular control was that both the governor and the legislative council had the power of veto over the bills of the lower assembly.

It follows that the appointed members of the government were from the "establishment" — the religious group in power, the important merchants, and other influential and wealthy groups. These people naturally opposed any change in the system which was supporting them in their positions of influence, and they usually advised the governor against acceding to any of the demands of any reforming element. The British government usually appointed the governor.

As a result, a conflict sprang up between the elected and appointed groups in the governments. In each colony, two main political groups emerged, one wishing to hold on to the current state of affairs (the conservatives), and the other demanding change (the reformers). The conservatives were generally known as the Tories.

The Tories usually held that the reformers were disloyal to the British Crown and wished to either introduce an American system of government, or even to join the U.S.A. The reformers countered, with some justice, that it had been the lack of reform which had caused the American Revolution, and that the attitude of the Tories was likely to cause a repetition in British North America.

It should be remembered that the reformers were opposed only to the existing form of colonial government; they knew that remaining in the British Empire was an economic advantage and had no quarrel with the British authorites apart from the unquestioning support of the governors by the Colonial Office. There was an additional political cause in the example of the recent (1832) political reform of the House of Commons in Britain. Further, immigrants from Britain after 1832 had experienced the social reforms which had followed the reform of the lower house there.

### ii. Economic
The construction of the Erie Canal (see above) had caused an economic depression. This, at first, had only affected Montreal and the fur trade. However, the southern movement of the fur trade had gradually affected both Upper and Lower Canada.

## b. Causes in Upper Canada
### i. Political
The governor usually followed a course acceptable to a group of Anglican financiers and merchants known as the Family Compact. A typical member was John Strachan, who was a bishop of the Church of England and a member of the executive council and the legislative council for twenty years before the rebellion. He, with the other members of the Family Compact, formed a tight oligarchy which controlled the political and economic affairs of the colony. The leader of the reform element was William Lyon Mackenzie, a Toronto editor, mayor of Toronto and elected to the legislative assembly.

### ii. Religious
The Protestant groups outside the Church of England were discriminated against, particularly in the matter of the Clergy Reserves, which had been established to support the clergy of all Protestant groups. Strachan supported the claims of his church that only it was permitted to use the proceeds from the Reserves. In this, he was bitterly opposed by leaders of the other Protestant groups, particularly Egerton Ryerson, the Methodist. The Presbyterians and Baptists also demanded reform in the matter of the Reserves.

### iii. Economic
There was the basic complaint that the Family Compact, through the governor, was running the economic life of the colony solely in its own interest. In addition, the agricultural community resented the Reserves system, by which one-seventh of the land in the colony was held undeveloped for religious financial support.

There was no return of proceeds from the Reserves for the construction of schools, roads and the other amenities necessary for the opening up of bush territory. On the other hand, the farmers pointed out, there was no shortage of funds for developments such as the Bank of Upper Canada and the Welland Canal.

### iv. Immediate Cause
The immediate cause of the rebellion in Upper Canada was the

refusal of the assembly to vote "supply" (of money) for the day-to-day running of the colony, in 1837. This led to the open break between the governor and the reform group (see Events Leading to the Rebellion, below).

## c. Causes in Lower Canada
### i. Political

Here, political authority was in the hands of the British governor, advised by a group of influential English and Church of England merchants, known as the Chateau Clique. Their system of control was practically the same as that exercised by the Family Compact in Upper Canada.

### ii. Ethnic

There was the aggravating factor in Lower Canada of the difference in ethnic background between the rulers and the ruled. This basic difference affected the political life of the colony (see above), but there was also a difference in economic aims between the two groups. Generally, in Lower Canada, the demand for reform included an element of demand for recognition of French Canada's real differences of culture and identity. Since the oligarchy was English in background, there was the suspicion that it intended to attempt to turn the French Canadians into a form of English Canadian. However, the French Canadian leaders took every opportunity to use the assembly, granted in the Constitutional Act of 1791, as a protection for their French heritage. At the first meeting in 1792, they had successfully forced admission of French as an official language for its proceedings and the official life of the colony.

The political leader of the reformers, during the period leading up to the rebellion, was Louis-Joseph Papineau, whose main motive was not merely democratic control, but popular French Canadian control. This eventually cost him the support of other reformers such as John Neilson, editor of the Quebec Gazette. On the other hand, Papineau's demands for popular control caused some of the French Canadian establishment — the upper clergy and the remaining seigneurs — to support the Chateau Clique.

### iii. Economic

The politico-economic group in power was expansionist in outlook. It wished to encourage immigration, build roads, and canals, and to finance this, proposed to use taxes based on land.

The French Canadians, however, were not in agreement with these aims. They were more interested in achieving a stable economic (and cultural) society, with dependable prices and markets for produce. They feared that the opening of schools and communications, together with immigration, would dilute the French Canadian identity.

In the matter of land tenure, in 1825 the British parliament had passed the Canada Land Tenures Act, which allowed the introduction of freehold, rather than seigneurial tenure. French Canadians were generally opposed to the implementation of this act, and the assembly fought a long delaying action against it. Further, the French Canadians wished the running of the colony to be financed out of trade, rather than land.

### iv. Religious
The causative effect of religion was that it was an extra element in the cleavage between the group in power and the mass of the population. The cleavage in Lower Canada can reasonably be said, without over-simplification, to have been based on political, ethnic, economic and religious differences between the French Canadians and the ruling English oligarchy.

### v. Immediate Cause
The immediate cause of the rebellion in Lower Canada was that after the presentation of the Ninety-Two Resolutions (see Events Leading to the Rebellion, below), Papineau appeared to be in imminent danger of arrest for high treason. His supporters then took to armed rebellion. This action, when discovered, was similarly supported by Mackenzie's supporters in Upper Canada (1837).

N.B. There were similar political and economic causes of discontent in the other colonies of British North America, but these took no part in the armed rebellion which occurred in Upper and Lower Canada.

## 2. Events Leading to the Rebellion
### a. In Lower Canada
The government in Lower Canada had its own source of revenue from land sales and customs duties. This made it semi-independent of the lower house in financial matters. Papineau knew that until the assembly controlled all income it would have no real power.

The government was prepared to allow this, provided that the assembly would permanently guarantee enough money for the salaries of all officials. Papineau found this unacceptable, on the grounds that there would be no popular control of these officials under such circumstances.

Concurrently, the ruling oligarchy feared French Canadian control of the government; not wishing to see the English minority subject to the political power of the majority. This was particularly true of the mercantile group, who realized that taxation for expansion would come to an end.

An effort to dispose of this difficulty, a proposed union of the two Canadas in 1822, had been bitterly resisted by the French Canadians, who had not seen this as a concession at all. In 1831, therefore, the British government finally agreed to give the assembly power over income and allowed the requirement of a permanent civil list to lapse.

By this time, however, Papineau's demands had gone beyond this, and the conciliatory offer was turned down. In 1834, Papineau tabled in the assembly a lengthy list of alleged grievances, generally known as the Ninety-Two Resolutions. He insisted that until these complaints were met, the reform element, then in the majority in the assembly, would refuse to vote money ("supply") to the executive.

In the same year, Lord Gosford had been sent out as governor. He began by offering places in the legislative council to the reformers, but would not go so far as to have a completely elected council. Papineau rejected this offer and maintained the blockade on supply.

In 1837, the British government made its position clear. In a statement by the Colonial Secretary, Lord John Russell, it turned down the demand for an elected legislative council. The statement, known as the Ten Resolutions, completely denied the possibility of responsible government (i.e., the governor only to act on the advice of ministers responsible to the people by being elected to the lower house). The statement went so far as to hold that the governor was entitled to dispose of revenue without an act of the assembly authorizing it.

This last resolution, to the reformers, came very close to the same "taxation without representation" which had helped to cause the American Revolution. The entire statement appeared to close the door to further reform by negotiation. It also coincided with an economic depression and unemployment.

Rioting took place in Montreal on November 7, 1837. Papineau, afraid that his presence was inflaming the rioters, planned to leave the area. The government took this to be a move on his part to spread the troubles in the outlying districts and decided to arrest him and other reform leaders.

This led to open hostilities and was thus the final cause of the rebellion in Lower Canada.

## b. In Upper Canada

The rebellion in Upper Canada can be traced back to the ejection from the assembly, soon after the War of 1812, of an American-born colonist, Barnabas Bidwell. His real crime had been his criticism of the Family Compact's handling of the colony's affairs. It was not until 1828 that U.S.-born settlers had the same civil rights as the other inhabitants of Upper Canada.

By 1824, Mackenzie was attacking the establishment in *The Colonial Advocate*. In 1826, the Tories destroyed his press. The reformers countered by electing him to the assembly. Like Papineau, he quickly saw that the crux of the issue was control of the public purse.

In 1831, the executive agreed to allow the assembly to control revenue in return for a guaranteed annual sum for officials' salaries, much as in Lower Canada. Like Papineau, Mackenzie decried this offer as leaving the government beyond the control of the assembly.

His declaration was, however, immoderate. The oligarchy had him expelled from the assembly for libel. Although a defiant populace re-elected him four times, on each occasion he was refused entry to his seat.

In 1834, however, there was a reform majority in the assembly; then he took his seat. The following year, he was elected (the first) mayor of Toronto. Unfortunately, as with Papineau, his demands began to disturb his more moderate supporters. Ryerson and Robert Baldwin, an influential Toronto lawyer, now refused to support his radical program which had just been displayed in Mackenzie's *Seventh Report on Grievances*, an attack on the oligarchy and land policy.

At this time, the British sent out Sir Francis Bond Head as governor. By inclination a conservative, he began, however, by inviting three moderate reformers, including Baldwin, to the executive council. Unfortunately, Bond Head soon showed that he did not feel obliged to accept the advice of his council.

As a result, all the council, including the Tories, resigned. The lower house supported the council's action and refused supply, coupling this with a demand for responsible government in that the council should be acceptable to the assembly — that is, the majority party in the assembly.

Bond Head replied by dissolving the assembly and calling an election. By a mixture of cajolery, bribes and threats he was able to ensure the return of an assembly favorable to his policies. (It should be remembered that this was in the days of open voting.)

So armed, he turned down any possibility of meeting any of the demands of the reformers, who now abandoned hope of any progress by following parliamentary procedure. The Ten Resolutions (see above) indicated that it would be pointless to expect any help from the British government.

The economic slump was followed by news of the uprising in Lower Canada. On hearing of it, Mackenzie mobilized his resources, and the disaffected farmers and artisans of the colony armed themselves and converged on Toronto.

## 3. Events of the Rebellion
### a. In Lower Canada

Skirmishes took place at St. Eustache, St. Denis and St. Charles. The rebels, however, were no match for the garrison of British regulars and were easily defeated. Within a very short time, the reform leaders were forced to flee to the U.S.A.

### b. In Upper Canada

The most important "battle" took place at Montgomery's Tavern in Toronto (roughly at the corner of Yonge and Eglinton today). Again, the untrained locals were easily dispersed by the uniformed troops. Mackenzie, too, was forced to take refuge in the U.S.A.

## 4. Results of the Rebellion

a. The reformers who had fled to the U.S.A. attempted to reorganize their forces in and from that country. However, although this was the beginning of a five-year period of extreme bad feeling between the U.S.A. and Britain, the U.S. government was not anxious to provoke a border war, and refused to become involved with supporting the rebels.

b. There were, however, a few border raids, as private ventures. These were easily disposed of, but were made the excuse for some local repression on the part of the British authorities in Upper Canada.

c. It was shown that the majority of Canadians, in both Canadas, preferred to believe that there were other methods of seeking redress and reform besides armed rebellion. The main local lesson was that the Catholic Church in Lower Canada was opposed to the introduction of true democracy, as, indeed, were many of the people themselves. In Upper Canada, it was shown that the British connection remained the paramount political fact.

d. Most important, the rebellion brought to the attention of the British parliament the fact that there were serious problems in British North America. As a result of the airing of the situation in the House of Commons, Lord Durham was sent out to enquire into and report on the rebellion and its causes.

# VI. Durham's Report

John Lambton, Earl of Durham, had been one of the leaders in the struggle for the First Reform Act (1832) in Britain. He was also close to Gibbon Wakefield and was under the influence of the latter's views on the colonies.

Wakefield and Durham were radical imperialists. That is, they believed that the allowance of self-government as soon as reasonable, to the colonies, plus free trade and assisted emigration, would make them both loyal and useful members of the Empire. There was, at this time, a considerable body of opinion in Britain which held that colonies were dangerous and expensive nuisances to the mother country and ought to be eliminated as soon as possible; the proponents of this attitude pointed to the British experience with the lost American colonies as proof.

The radical imperialists, however, by no means advocated complete independence, and there was no intention by Durham to offer this when he arrived in May, 1838, accompanied by Wakefield.

The investigation rapidly came to the obvious conclusion that the root of the problems was in the disputes between the assemblies and the oligarchies. In particular, Durham was greatly influenced by Robert Baldwin's advice that responsible government would be the answer to this problem.

Under this system, which, after all, was that enjoyed by the inhabitants in the home country, the governor would be working in cooperation with the expressed will of the people (i.e., at the most recent election for the assembly), rather than ruling as an autocrat advised by a remote oligarchy. Baldwin warned that the only alternative to responsible government, in the temper of the times, would be direct military rule from Britain.

Durham was prepared to accept this position for Upper Canada, particularly since it did not mean complete independence. He would not, however, recommend it for Lower Canada, since this would result in the English minority coming under the power of the French Canadians. He tended to see the problem in Lower Canada as being completely involved with the ethnic differences. He was also doubtful whether allowing the French Canadian reformers to take power would be in the better interests of the colony, having regard to their views on the development of industry.

Durham reached his final conclusions within a mere six months, and embodied these in his report, below. He was relieved of his authority in September, 1838, when the British government refused to endorse his summary punishment of some of the rebels in transporting them to the West Indies. His report was published in 1839.

## Terms and their Implementation

1. He recommended that Upper and Lower Canada should be united to form one colony. Since English Canadians had, at the time, a tiny but growing majority in the Canadas, taken together, French Canadians were opposed to the idea of union. The English minority in Quebec, understandably, was favorably inclined.

The British government accepted Durham's recommendations and at once enacted the Act of Union (1840), the union to take effect in 1841. Perhaps a longer period of consideration by the British parliament might have resulted in a different allocation of seats in the lower, elected, house; as it was, these seats were allocated equally to Upper and Lower Canada. The influx of settlers from English-speaking areas later demonstrated that the French Canadians had a preponderance of seats in proportion to their numbers of population. At the time, however, the English-speaking Canadians received more seats than their numbers would entitle them to.

The Act of Union set up a government consisting of the British Crown, represented by a governor sent from Britain, ruling with two houses. The lower house, the legislative assembly, was completely elected and half the members were from each of the two Canadas. The upper house, the legislative council, was intended to be appointed, rather on the lines of the British House of Lords, but by 1856 it, too, was an elected body.

2. The British government refused to act upon Durham's recommendation of responsible government, and the Act of Union makes no mention of it. It was understood that this was an attainable aim, in the unspecified future. The main target of reformers in Canada after the establishment of the new system under the Act of Union was the inauguration of responsible government as soon as possible.

The Upper Canada Tories, in any case, were opposed to responsible government, saying that Durham had been wrongly advised in this matter, and that its inception would amount to a reward for treason.

The result was a compromise. The British government was itself a Liberal government, the members of which had their own recent memories of the evils of oligarchic government. The governor was exhorted, but not commanded, to choose advisers who represented the feelings of the majority. This did not necessarily mean that they had been elected to office, however. He was to co-operate with the lower house, at most, but he was not required to follow its advice, nor even that of his executive council, which remained responsible solely to his office and not in any way to the people or the assembly.

3. Durham also made recommendations as to improvements in the methods of local government. (The British had amended their own system in 1835). These were generally carried out.

4. Durham recommended that a railway should be built from the interior, entirely on British territory, to the all-weather port of Halifax. It was generally agreed that this intercolonial railway should be built, but difficulties of financing at the colonial level prevented its completion until the evolution of Canada as a confederation.

5. Durham recommended the British system of allowing financial measures to be brought into the assembly only by a minister of the Crown. This became the established practice with the arrival of responsible government.

6. He recommended that the new governments in British North

America should have a much greater area of responsibility. Instead of having areas of authority delegated to them, the colonies should be presumed to have authority over all matters except stated fields.

The latter should only be at the imperial level, leaving the colonial government self-sufficient as regards local matters. The few imperial matters to be left to the British government were defence, foreign trade, external affairs, colonial constitutions (which included the rights and duties of the governors) and the allocation of public lands.

In the last resort, Britain ought to be allowed to legislate in internal Canadian matters, however, and a final safety measure, from the British point of view, would be that the Canadian government would not be able to amend its own constitution.

These recommendations came gradually into effect as they became prominent in the political development; not all, however, were achieved. For instance, by Canada's own request, parts of the current constitution can still only be amended by an act of the British parliament.

N.B. Relations with the Canadian Indians remained within the authority of the British government.

## VII. The Arrival of Responsible Government in Canada

The first governor of Canada was Lord Sydenham. He knew that, if he were to succeed in his double task of pacifying Canada and establishing a stable government for the new colony, he had to have a majority in the assembly at his disposal.

This meant, in the first instance, that he would have to organize his own party and be his own party leader. He began by arranging a loan from Britain and using it to reduce the internal debt and to start public works.

However, Papineau's successor as head of the Lower Canada reformers, Louis LaFontaine, was not prepared to co-operate with the governor, who had invited opposition by declining to have French Canadians on his executive council.

At the same time, Robert Baldwin realized that Sydenham had no real intention of introducing full responsible government, and maintained his demands for it in the assembly.

The result was that Sydenham sought to have the assembly endorse a series of resolutions introduced by a man called Harrison. These resolutions stipulated that the governor was responsible solely to the British Crown, while agreeing that his chief advisers ought to have the confidence of the people.

This did not appease Baldwin or LaFontaine. The impasse was

solved by the untimely death of Sydenham two weeks after the introduction of the Harrison resolutions.

Sydenham's successor, Sir Charles Bagot, had been advised by British Prime Minister, Sir Robert Peel, to adopt a more conciliatory attitude towards the French Canadian leaders. On reaching Canada, he soon decided that he would not follow Sydenham's policies. In any case, Sydenham's personal party had collapsed with his death.

Bagot's attitude was, that since LaFontaine and Baldwin controlled the lower house between them, they ought to form the executive council also. But Bagot had been ordered by the British government to refuse responsible government, and he knew that the two reform leaders were committed to its introduction.

There was the complication that although he was to conciliate French Canada, he was under orders not to give any real power to the French Canadian leaders; in this matter, of course, he was supported by the Upper Canada Tories.

However, Bagot knew what was necessary. In September, 1842, he was able to prevail upon Baldwin and LaFontaine to take office. At the same time, he advised London that Baldwin was the actual political leader of the country. It can be reasonably be said that Bagot's action was an acceptance of the principle of responsible government.

Again, however, the office of governor changed hands at a crucial time. Bagot fell ill and was forced to return to Britain. His successor, Sir Charles Metcalfe, held reactionary views, and deadlock followed.

Metcalfe was quite certain that his duty was to resist responsible government which he interpreted as surrender of the authority of the Crown and the authority of the mother country. Nor was he prepared to place his own opinions below those of any elected person or body, and, in his view, his terms of office did not require him to do so.

A collision could not be avoided. LaFontaine and Baldwin resigned in late 1843, and the colony fell under the personal rule of the governor, who was unable to command a majority in the lower house.

After a year of this, Metcalfe called a general election. He went beyond the intended bounds of his office by taking a personal part in the campaigns. At the same time, the Tories raised the old bogeys of treason and disloyalty in reference to the reform group. Ryerson came out in support of the governor. As a result, the latter gained a slight majority.

Again, however, health became a factor. Metcalfe returned to Britain in 1845, to die. Canada had still not attained responsible government.

Events in Britain now affected the issue. The Liberal party (which had been out of office since 1841) returned to power in 1846. It at once adopted a policy of free trade. Since this was an actual abandonment of power over colonial trade, it implied a certain amount of abandonment of power over colonial government.

The Liberal Colonial Secretary was Lord Grey, who was married to Lord Durham's sister. Grey was also a radical imperialist. He was plainly committed to allowing responsible government.

Remarkably, Nova Scotia was the colony to benefit first. The reformers had continued to work for reform through normal channels, and had not taken part in the 1837 rebellion. The reform element there was led by the Halifax editor, Joseph Howe.

Howe, in his newspaper, had made the reasonable demand for reform and responsible government in a series of articles, known as the *Four Open Letters* (1839). In these he had pointed out that Canadians were asking for no more than was already enjoyed by citizens in England.

The lieutenant-governor of Nova Scotia was Sir John Harvey. Grey's first directive to him made it clear that there was a new attitude to Canada in the Colonial Office. It stated that there was no longer any intention to govern the colonies in British North America except according to the will of the majority of the inhabitants.

Nova Scotia went to the polls in 1847 and elected a majority of reformers. An attempt was made to form a government without them, but it failed to survive a non-confidence motion. In accordance with British practice, Harvey then invited Howe and the reformers to form a government, thus inaugurating responsible government in British North America.

In Canada, Grey had appointed Lord Elgin governor to replace Metcalfe. Elgin was married to Durham's daughter. Grey's instructions to Elgin were much the same as to Harvey. If the majority of the public elected reformers, then Elgin would have to accept the advice of the reformers in running the colony.

A reform majority was returned in 1847, and Baldwin and LaFontaine were invited to organize a government. The principle of responsible government in Canada was not, however, tested until 1849. In that year, the assembly passed the Rebellion Losses Bill. This statute was extremely unacceptable in Tory areas. Since it compensated people in the former Lower Canada who had suffered destruction of property during the rebellion, without any clear stipulation as to the cause of damage, the Tories held that the Bill was a reward for rebellion, and inspired by revenge on the part of the surviving French Canadian reformers.

Both Elgin and the British government felt that parts of the statute were unfair, but also felt that the principle of responsible government required Elgin to sign the Bill.

Rioting followed the enactment of the statute. Parliament buildings in Montreal were burned down in April, 1849. However, Elgin maintained that he was required to assent to the legislation placed before him by his advisers, in accordance with the principle of responsible government. It can reasonably be said that responsible government had been won by the working together of reformers from both the main ethnic communities in the colony.

## The Webster-Ashburton Treaty, 1842

The boundary between Maine and New Brunswick had never been clearly set out. The area was not settled, but in the era of bad feeling after 1837, lumbermen from either side of the frontier clashed. In 1841, Lord Ashburton was dispatched from Britain to negotiate with the U.S.A.

The discussions were marked by extreme bad faith on each side. Both parties believed they were in possession of original sources which proved the other's case to be correct, but both concealed the information.

The U.S. negotiator was Daniel Webster, the Secretary of State. In 1842, an agreement was made in which practically all the U.S. claims were met. The treaty was unpopular in both countries. However, it did perpetuate the system, set up after the War of 1812, of settling disputes by negotiation. At the same time, sufficient land was left for the construction of the intercolonial railway when capital became available.

# VIII. Canada, 1849 to Confederation

## 1. The Economy

The old colonial system ended with the advent of free trade and the repeal of the Navigation Acts by the British government between 1846 and 1849. Practically all the preferences enjoyed by Canadian merchants within the Empire were lost. It was plain that reorganization of the colonies' economy was crucial.

The first reaction, by Montreal mercantile elements, was to ask for annexation by the U.S.A. This attitude was not well supported outside this group.

There was some early talk of a federation of the British North American colonies, but this was too far in advance of its time. The more practical step was to extend trade with the U.S.A., and the best apparent way to do this was to inaugurate some measure of free trade (i.e., reciprocity) between the two.

Generally, the basic desire of the U.S.A. was to use the Canadian inshore fishing grounds; the Canadians were chiefly interested in developing a U.S. market for natural products. Negotiations to this end were left in the hands of Lord Elgin.

In 1854 he completed the Reciprocity Treaty. This called for free navigation, by the two parties, of the Great Lakes and the St. Lawrence, joint access to the inshore fisheries, and free trade in natural products between the U.S.A. and British North America.

This treaty (which was signed by Great Britain and the U.S.A.) saved the Canadian economy, although much of the trade of the colonies remained with the mother country (from one-half in Canada to almost 70 per cent in the Maritimes). It was also of importance in that, for the first time, the British North American colonial area had been dealt with as a unit, rather than a set of individual colonies. As such, it foreshadowed Confederation.

Another economic development which showed the increased stature of British North America was the enactment in 1859, in Canada, of a protectionist tariff which discriminated against British goods. Although the British government indicated its opposition, the implication of responsible political government is independence in internal economic matters and the British were forced to accept this principle. One minor economic advance in 1854 was the abolition of the Clergy Reserves.

## 2. Railways

In the 1850's, there was rapid economic expansion. Partially responsible was the increase in population in the St. Lawrence basin — to almost one million in Canada West by 1851, with a clear majority over Canada East (which included an English Canadian minority, in any case).

The expansion also caused a demand for railways, which involved both financiers and politicians. The Minister of Finance, Galt, hoped to rebuild the old St. Lawrence-Great Lakes economic system with a British North American group of railways.

The main requirement, however, was the intercolonial railway recommended by Durham. The Grand Trunk Railway was the main attempt to put this project through; it was intended to run from Sarnia to Halifax on British soil. The builders and capital were largely from the mother country.

The section of track in East and West Canada was complete by 1860, but east of Montreal the company ran into difficulties. It finally ran out of capital and the British government declined to pour further money into it. The individual maritime colonies had no hope of completing the line themselves. Eventually, a route to the Atlantic was made available, but it crossed U.S. territory and the port was Portland, Maine.

Railways were inextricably involved with politics and public funds during this period, because the public purse was the only one big enough to finance railway development. Railways were begun with optimistic estimates of total cost; construction, first, and actual operation, later, proved financially difficult or unrewarding, and colonial funds were diverted into both.

A significant amount of corruption and extravagance was a natural result. However, railways were constructed — thirty times as many miles in 1860 as in 1850 — and they did make a great contribution to the opening of the colonial west and north, to say nothing of establishing a basis for heavy industry in the railway centers.

In the same way, they caused something of a cultural and social breakthrough by permitting travel and ending the isolation of the frontier townships. They also provided the basis for the political union of the eastern colonies which followed later and showed the medium by which the far west might be brought into it.

## 3. The West

The area west and north of Lake Huron was almost entirely unexploited at this time. It was clear that if it could be populated and organized, it would provide raw materials for the older areas and a market for finished products.

At the start of the period, however, the entire west was the domain of the Hudson's Bay Company, whose policy was against colonizing for agriculture. However, the Anglo-American crisis over the Oregon Territory's boundary, which resulted in the extension of the 49th parallel boundary to the Pacific (1846), had directed Canadian attention to the far west.

Another development was the gold strike (1858) on the Fraser River in what is now British Columbia. This caused a rush of miners from California, rather than from British North America, and the danger of an internal and popular demand for annexation of British Columbia by the U.S.A.

The only colony of any note on the Canadian prairies was that at Fort Garry (later Winnipeg), which was something of an island of settlement in mid-continent. However, the territory to the south had been filling up, and in 1858 the State of Minnesota was organized. It was clear that the politicians of that state were interested in northern expansion into Canadian territory and this could only be resisted if the British could extend practical authority and communications to the west.

# IX. The Confederation of Canada, 1867

## 1. Causes

    a. Durham's intercolonial railway had not been built. The hostility of the U.S.A. towards Britain in 1865 (see below) showed the drastic economic and strategic need for such a railway. However, no individual colony had enough financial resources to complete its own section in the Maritimes, and the contemporary British attitude, government and private, was that financial help could only be offered to a much more solid organization than the government of one small colony.

b. In the same way, it became apparent that an Atlantic-Pacific railway on British soil was both desirable and practicable. There was, however, clearly no one to finance such a project apart from the existing governments in British North America, and individually they had no hope of either raising the capital themselves or persuading the British to underwrite it.

c. The problem of developing the Prairies (see above) depended upon transport and communications. If these were not organized, it might well be that Canada would lose her room for western expansion by default, but there was no single authority capable of undertaking this project. The danger of annexation made the problem the more urgent.

d. In the same way, British Columbia appeared likely to be lost because of lack of a unified British North America and a transport link across the Prairies.

e. There was a climate of Anglo-American hostility at the end of the U.S. Civil War in 1865. Canada would naturally be involved in any hostilities or hostile measures that might ensue, as in 1812. It was obvious that the colonies would be better able to handle defence problems as one group rather than isolated groups. There were also some grounds for belief that the British government was somewhat indifferent to Canadian defence problems, on the grounds of expense. In fact, there was a body of opinion in Britain which advocated federation so that the colonies would be independent in defence costs.

There were many reasons for, and some manifestations of, this Anglo-American climate of hostility. The Union had won the U.S. Civil War, but the British government had supported the Confederacy in the early stages of the war, although it had not gone so far as to recognize it as a separate nation.

In 1861, the U.S. government had removed two Confederate diplomats from a British steamer, the *Trent*. The British government had protested and forced the Union to allow the diplomats to proceed to Britain.

In the early stages of the war, the British had allowed the *Alabama*, a warship under construction, to escape despite Union protests and it sank many Union vessels.

In October, 1864, a group of Confederate sympathizers raided a bank in St. Albans, Vermont, for funds for the Confederacy. It was clear that they had used Canada as their base of operations. A Montreal court allowed the raiders to escape punishment on a technicality, and the Union was outraged.

Some hostile acts took place; others were feared. The 1854 Reciprocity Treaty had been abrogated by the U.S. Senate in 1865. There was talk in the U.S. of once more putting warships on the Great Lakes.

More important, it lay within the power of the U.S.A. at any time to cut off Canada's winter access to the Atlantic by the simple method of prohibiting use of the Portland extension to the Grand Trunk Railway. At the very least, the "in-bond" privileges of Canada on that stretch could be withdrawn. By this concession, Canadian goods for export to Europe were loaded in Canada, and the freight-cars then travelled over the U.S. section of the line unopened, free from all U.S. customs duties and tariffs.

In addition, the Fenian movement was becoming active in the northern states. This was an organization of Irish-Americans which still retained hostile feelings towards Britain, the most recent cause being the poor British handling of the 1844 famine in Ireland.

To show their gratitude to their adopted country, these Irish-Americans proposed to capture Canada and make a gift of it to the U.S.A., thereby obtaining some form of revenge on Britain. There was no real fear, at the time, that the movement was backed by Washington, though the movement was training openly.

f. The most important cause of Confederation, however, was the political deadlock within Canada itself. The Union Act of 1841 had not been a success, mainly because it was based on the ethnic difference between English and French Canada. Although the aims of French Canadian and English reformers had been temporarily the same in the 1830's, once responsible government had been attained these two groups developed separately.

When, in the 1850's, it became apparent that the English population of former Upper Canada increasingly exceeded that of French Canada, a demand grew that the assembly should be organized on a basis of representation by population ("rep by pop"), rather than on a 50-50 basis.

This suggestion was, of course, bitterly resisted by French Canadians, for they feared that as a minority they might well lose their rights as regards education, language and religion. They objected, moreover, that "rep by pop" had not been an issue when the French population had exceeded the English.

The leader of the "rep by pop" group was George Brown, editor of the Toronto newspaper, *The Globe*. He was established as the real reform leader in Canada West after Robert Baldwin left the political scene in 1851. As a Presbyterian and a professed anti-Catholic, he was resented by the French Canadians in the assembly.

As a result, the latter began an unlikely and uncertain alliance with the English Tories in the lower house. The Tories were, in any case, more interested in commercial expansion than reform of the constitution. The Conservative party, formed of these two groups, had emerged by 1854; the English Canadian element was led by John A. Macdonald and the French Canadian by Georges Etienne Cartier.

The former felt that the Act of Union could operate provided that the economic climate was favorable. He also knew that he himself could not hope for political power at the time, except as part of the structure of a joint Tory-French Canadian group.

Cartier's motive for the alliance was protection of the French Canadian identity. This had the effect of making the unity of the group lowest whenever sectional differences arose in the assembly.

The Macdonald-Cartier group assumed power in 1854. During its period in office, both the seigneurial land tenure system and the Clergy Reserves were done away with, and the Canada section of the Grand Trunk Railway was put through. These successes, however, did not remove the basic defects of the party structure. Macdonald himself slowly lost his chances of individual leadership as he refused to consider "rep by pop", an attitude which proved an impossible handicap for him in Canada West. Finally, the administration fell, over the choice of the site for the national capital.

Brown was no more lucky in retaining power. The only way in which his party could keep an uncertain majority in the assembly was by coalition with a small group of French Canadian nationalists, the Parti Rouge. When his administration failed, some of his followers (the "Clear Grits") took the view that the union of the two Canadas had failed, and should be abolished.

Brown was more moderate, and put forward the idea of a federation with the source of power at the local level, much as in the U.S. constitution, with a federal government in charge of national matters such as defence and external relations.

Cartier and Macdonald then said that they were willing to cooperate with Brown's scheme, provided the Maritimes were included. (Another influential politician, Galt, had, in 1858, thrown in his lot with the Macdonald-Cartier group provided they would give some attention to the possibility of a federal program.)

There was some urgency by this time. Relations between Britain and the U.S.A. were becoming strained in the early 1860's, yet the inability of any government to maintain a majority had prevented definite policies, even in defence. After 1862, four successive governments in the Canadas had an average life of six months each.

Succeeding elections showed no real change in the electorate's wishes or the party alignments. Clearly, it was the system that was at fault; a new constitutional system was obviously necessary.

## 2. Events Leading to Confederation

a. In June, 1864, George Brown, the Grit leader, formed a committee to look into the prospects of federation. On the same day that the committee reported to the assembly that federation was preferable, the Macdonald-Cartier administration fell. The committee found that either a federation of Canada West and Canada East, or a wider federation including all British North America, was desirable.

b. As a result, Brown then declared that he was willing to enter a coalition government with any Tory group which would commit itself to the federation program. Macdonald took Brown up on his offer (June, 1864), but both men realized that without Cartier's support, progress would not be possible.

The latter, however, realized well enough that some such development was necessary; he was now entirely convinced that the French Canadian identity would be better protected within a federation. The three political leaders were joined in their administration by Galt.

c. At the same time, the Maritime colonies were also moving towards the same goal, although limited to a federation of the Atlantic colonies. They had gone as far as to organize a meeting at Charlottetown (September, 1864) to investigate the prospects of such a move. The coalition government in Canada thereupon asked if it might send a delegation to this meeting, to observe and address it on the possibility of the wider federation of British North America as a whole. This was acceptable to the conference's organizers.

At the Charlottetown Conference, the delegation from Canada presented its case so well that the Atlantic group decided that a further conference should be held, to go into the matter in detail.

d. This second conference took place at Quebec the following month, and the work centred on the division of powers between the two levels of government, provincial and national. The U.S. Civil War, brought on by the question of states' rights versus federal rights, was being fought; to Macdonald's mind, it could have been avoided if the fathers of the U.S. Constitution had provided for a strong central government.

He was unable to convince the delegates from all of the provinces, although the majority were for a system with the major power at the center; in particular, the Atlantic colonies and Quebec were sensitive to any loss of autonomy.

Finally, all were persuaded to favor some form of national federation except Newfoundland and Prince Edward Island, which dropped out at that point. (N.B. It was at this stage that the U.S. Senate gave notice of the abrogation of the Reciprocity Treaty. It was also the period when the possibility of Fenian raids was most feared.)

e. In February, 1865, Macdonald and Cartier presented their plans to the Canada legislature. Cartier pacified the French Canadians. Galt pointed out the commercial advantages and similarly pacified the English minority in Quebec. Macdonald showed the dangers which were likely if some progress towards federation were not made. Brown, however, pointed out the internal dangers of the political deadlock within Canada itself. The result was that the Quebec Resolutions passed the Canada legislature by a majority of three to one. This was the only time that the confederation of Canada was formally placed before the people of the most populous part of the proposed new country.

f. In Nova Scotia, however, the temper of the people was running against confederation. There was local suspicion of the bigger colony of Canada, which even the offer of the completion of the intercolonial railway could not dispel. When Joseph Howe himself declared that he found confederation unacceptable, it was clear that passage of the Quebec Resolutions through the legislature was, at best, doubtful. As a result, the leader, Tupper, decided not to risk introducing them, in case they should be defeated.

g. In New Brunswick, the confederation interest, led by Tilley, was defeated in the elections of March, 1865. It seemed, then, that the scheme would fail.

h. External events caused a reversal of the tide against confederation later in 1865. In New Brunswick, the governor received orders from Britain that he was to work actively for confederation. He called a new election at the first opportunity, in early 1866.

During the election campaign, the Fenian threat became real. Tilley was returned to office with his program of confederation.

i. Something similar, and for the same reasons, took place at the same time in Nova Scotia. Tupper introduced the matter formally into the legislature, which endorsed confederation and committed itself to sending delegates to the next conference.

j. The final conference was held in London, and started in December, 1866. The Quebec Resolutions were still the foundation of confederation, but, to safeguard the participation of the attending Maritime colonies, the intercolonial railroad was guaranteed and the financial incentives to the Maritimes were increased. (Prince Edward Island, Newfoundland and British Columbia did not send delegates to the London conference.)

k. In March, 1867, the British North America Act (1867), generally taken to be the basic statute in the Canadian constitution, was passed by the Parliament of the United Kingdom.

l. As a result, the Dominion of Canada came into being on July 1, 1867.

# X. The Canadian Constitution — A Summary

## 1. Historical Background

a. It was drawn up shortly after the American Civil War. This had been fought to decide state vs. federal rights, and the Fathers of Confederation were determined to avoid a similar war in Canada.

b. There was already a minority group in Canada when the British North America Act was drawn up.

c. Modern methods of transport and communication were in use.

d. Parliamentary and responsible government already existed in Canada.

## 2. General

The British North America Act (1867) is an act of the British Parliament. It requires that Canada shall have 'a Constitution similar in principle to that of Great Britain'. It also lays down that the government shall consist of the Crown and a legislature of two houses, at Ottawa. The lower House is to be elected, the Senate is to be appointed for life. (This has since been amended to 75 years of age.)

## 3. The Crown

a. "The Executive Government and authority of and over Canada is...vested in the Queen". (The Queen referred to is still Queen Victoria.)

b. Her duties in her absence are carried out by the Governor-General.

c. The Crown selects a Governor-General on the advice of the Government of Canada. He traditionally occupies the post for five years, but this term can be extended by agreement.

d. His advisers must be members of the Queen's Privy Council for Canada (see below), of which body federal Cabinet members are automatically members.

e. His main governmental duty is to summon, prorogue or dissolve Parliament on the recommendation of his advisers. He also gives, at the commencement of each session of Parliament, the Speech from the Throne — an outline of government policy written by the Prime Minister and Cabinet.

f. The royal assent is the final stage in a bill becoming law.

g. The Crown acts as prosecutor in all criminal cases.

## 4. The Executive

    a. The executive branch of the government is directed by the Prime Minister.

    b. He is the leader of the political party with the majority of seats in the House of Commons. He selects the Cabinet from the members of his own party in the House of Commons, usually plus one Senator. He decides on the order of business in the House of Commons.

    c. His term of office is up to five years. He may be re-elected without limit.

    d. He may be forced out of office if the majority in the Commons votes against one of his party's major proposals, or if there is a successful vote of non-confidence in the Commons. His calling for an election after these two circumstances is not required by law, but is based on custom and tradition. This system is the basis of responsible government.

## 5. The Legislature

    Consists of the Crown, Senate and the Commons who exist to make laws for "peace, good order and good government" in any matters not exclusively assigned to the provinces.

### The Commons

    i. Members are elected by popular vote. The number of voters required to elect a member varies widely across Canada.

    ii. Money bills must begin in the Commons.

    iii. Since Cabinet members (except Senators) and the Prime Minister must be members of this House, it is the most influential and powerful chamber.

### The Senate

    i. There are 102 Senators, allocated by geographical division.

    ii. Senators are appointed for life by the Governor-General on the advice of the Cabinet in power.

    iii. The approval of the Senate is required before a Commons bill goes for royal assent.

    iv. There is dispute as to whether the Senate may amend a money bill.

    v. The Cabinet is not responsible to it. Seats in it are often used as a reward for services to a political party. Since Senators are not elected, they cannot claim to represent the will of the people. The Senate tends to be cautious and conservative, and usually does not oppose the Commons in important issues. As a result of these circumstances, the Senate has much less power and influence than the Commons.

## 6. The Judiciary
a. Parliament is empowered to set up a Court of Appeal (The Supreme Court) and any additional courts.

b. The Supreme Court consists of a Chief Justice (also acts as Deputy Governor-General) and eight Puisne Justices, appointed by the Governor-General on the advice of government in power, removable by the Governor-General on request of the Senate and Commons. Justices retire at 75.

c. The Supreme Court acts as a general appeal court for Canada in civil and criminal cases. It can be required by the Governor-General to advise on any question he refers to it.

d. Since 1952, its judgments have been final and conclusive. (Before 1952 the final court of appeal for Canadians was the Judicial Committee of the Privy Council, in London.)

e. A corollary of the latter circumstance is that the Supreme Court now interprets the Canadian constitution.

## 7. Other Features of Government
### a. The Opposition
i. The opposition is that group of members in the Commons whose policy usually differs from that of the majority party. Its official name is Her Majesty's Loyal Opposition.

ii. The leader of the opposition is the head of the second largest party in the Commons and is salaried.

iii. Its duties are to check the proposals of the party in power, persuade it to accept amendments to its bills, and attempt to replace it.

### b. The Speaker of the House of Commons
Acts as chairman of the Commons (except when it goes into committee). He is nominated by the majority party for the life of Parliament. His duty is to see that the rules of debate and procedure are followed. The Senate, similarly, has a speaker.

### c. The Cabinet
i. The Cabinet directs the executive branch of the government under the leadership of the Prime Minister.

ii. All except Senators are directly elected by the people. A Cabinet nominee not already an M.P. is traditionally elected as soon as possible after his appointment.

iii. All, except in emergency, are selected by the Prime Minister from the majority party in the House of Commons.

iv. It meets several times each week, with the Prime Minister as chairman. Since it decides the order of business for the Commons, and since most legislation is proposed by Cabinet members, the Cabinet tends to dominate the legislative branch of government.

v. The Cabinet traditionally resigns with the Prime Minister.

vi. The Cabinet is directly responsible to the electorate via the House of Commons (cabinet responsibility). All members must agree publicly with Cabinet decisions or resign (cabinet solidarity). Ministers take individual responsibility for mistakes within their departments (ministerial responsibility).

vii. Decisions of the Cabinet may be issued as orders of the Governor-General in the Queen's Privy Council for Canada (Orders-in-Council). This ensures speed and security in wartime, and avoids wasting the time of Parliament on lesser business contracts, appointments, etc., in peacetime. It could be said that excessive use of orders-in-council might be a threat to democracy.

### d. The Queen's Privy Council for Canada

The Queen's Privy Council for Canada consists of some 80 members, mainly present and former federal ministers. It does not meet as a body. Its constitutional place as adviser to the Governor-General is taken by the Cabinet in power, whose members are sworn into the Council for life.

## 8. Other Features of the Canadian Constitution or System

### a. Amendments

In 1949, at Canadian request, the British Parliament passed an amendment to the B.N.A. Act by which the Canadian Parliament may amend its own constitution, except for those sections on provincial rights, education and language. A standing committee in Canada has been considering further amending procedure since 1950.

### b. Bill of Rights

This is a federal Act passed in 1960. It has no effect on provincial governments and merely drew attention to rights already enjoyed by Canadians and pointed out the responsibilities of these freedoms.

## 9. Provincial Governments

a. The Crown is represented in provincial legislatures by a Lieutenant-Governor, appointed by the Governor-General. He is required to act on the advice of the provincial cabinet except where this will cause conflict with the federal government.

    b. The legislature consists of one elected house (Quebec, however originally had a bi-cameral legislature). It may be dissolved by the Lieutenant-Governor on the advice of the provincial Premier. The Premier and Cabinet must resign when they no longer enjoy majority support in the legislature (responsible government).

### Exclusive Rights of Provinces

    i. Provinces may amend their own constitutions, except that they may not interfere with the office of Lieutenant-Governor.

    ii. They have the right to tax within the province. They have other rights specified by the B.N.A. Act including, in particular, jurisdiction over education and official languages, and in general, all matters of a purely provincial nature.

    iii. The federal government retains those powers (residual powers) not specifically given to provincial governments.

    iv. The federal government has power to disallow any provincial law which it feels clashes with federal law or is against the interests of Canada as a whole. This power has not been used since 1943.

    v. Except in wartime, the B.N.A. Act has been interpreted to limit the power of the federal government and to expand the powers of the provincial governments. This has been done by interpreting widely the section which allows provinces to legislate on "property and civil rights within the province", and interpreting narrowly federal power to "make all laws for the peace, order and good government of Canada".

# XI. Macdonald's Administration, 1867-1873

## 1. Internal

    Canada's first Prime Minister was Sir John A. Macdonald. Before long, his government consisted entirely of Conservatives. Canada West and East became Ontario and Quebec, with Galt and Cartier continuing to work with Macdonald.

### a. Completing the Nation

    i. Nova Scotia was still a reluctant member of Confederation. Newfoundland, Prince Edward Island and British Columbia were not in at all. (British Columbia and Vancouver Island had merged in 1866.)

Indeed, in the latter, the inhabitants were overwhelmingly U.S. citizens.

Nova Scotia's provincial legislature had an overwhelmingly anti-Confederation majority, led by Joseph Howe. Howe was forced to come to terms with Canada, however, when he was unable to negotiate a commercial treaty with the U.S.A.

In 1869, Macdonald persuaded Howe to accept a new financial agreement and a cabinet post for himself. The province received a further $140,000, and the separatist movement there gradually ceased.

ii. Prince Edward Island passed into the financial doldrums in the closing years of the 1860's. The main cause was its attempts to "go it alone" in the construction of a railway. It became clear that this was impossible without external financial aid.

The federal government offered to take over the island's railway responsibilities and, more important, guaranteed to obtain all the land necessary for completion of the line in the province. This, in 1873, finally persuaded Prince Edward Island to enter Confederation.

The federal government made two additional promises. An annual subsidy would be paid to the provincial government, and the federal government would guarantee some form of communication with the mainland.

iii. Newfoundland continued to resist federation with Canada and remained a British colony, with varying constitutions and status, until 1949, when it became a Canadian province.

iv. The West, administered by the Hudson's Bay Company, presented four problems. These were:

1. The company wanted compensation for any rights given up to the federal government.
2. There were no modern communications across the area, which, in any case, had only one permanent settlement of any size, the Red River Colony.
3. The U.S.A. appeared likely to have an interest in expansion into the same area.
4. The population, mostly Métis, did not particulary wish to join Canada.

The Hudson's Bay Company was bought out in 1869. The price was the grant of a wide expanse of land elsewhere, 45,000 acres around its posts, and $1,500,000 in cash. Regrettably, these arrangements were arrived at without consulting the inhabitants of these lands; the Métis felt, as a result, that their way of life and property were being endangered.

When surveyors from Canada started to divide their farms on a square survey, they feared their lands would be taken away. Louis Riel became their spokesman and they formed a government to defend their interest.

William McDougall, Macdonald's intended governor for the area, was refused entry by the Métis. Riel then sent a delegation to discuss the future of the region with the Canadian government.

There was a Canadian minority in the area, however, which refused to support him. In a show of authority, Riel caused one of them, Thomas Scott, to be shot on charges of striking his guards and insubordination.

This action aggravated and changed the tenor of the attitude of the rest of Canada. English Canada demanded that Riel be brought to trial as soon as possible. Quebec, however, had some sympathy with Riel, on the grounds that they had had difficulty with the English in preserving their own identity.

As a result, the country faced its first ethnic crisis as well as a serious situation in the West. Finally, Macdonald decided to meet a delegation from the Red River Colony to work out an arrangement whereby it might enter Confederation. The terms were set out in the Manitoba Act (1870).

By this, the Province of Manitoba was brought into existence. It was to have the same institutions and rights as the founding provinces. The undeveloped areas remained under the control of the federal government, but the Métis land titles in existence were recognized. The understanding was that the unsettled areas were to be used for settlers and railways under the sponsorship of the federal government.

As with Prince Edward Island, the federal government gave a large financial subsidy. Roman Catholic schools and the French language were guaranteed within the province for those concerned.

At the same time, Macdonald sent some militia west both to arrest Riel and to demonstrate to the U.S.A. the Canadian commitment on the Prairies. The British supported him by sending a force of regulars with the expedition. Riel, however, slipped across the border to the U.S.A. The new province gradually established itself, and the ethnic division in the East over the problem gradually assumed smaller proportions.

v. British Columbia, with the impetus gone from the gold rush, was heavily in debt, and the danger of annexation by the U.S.A. was as strong as ever.

A group, led by Amor de Cosmos, journeyed east to Ottawa to negotiate terms for entry into Confederation. These were finally established as was the usual financial subsidy and the federal promise of a transcontinental railroad to be completed within ten years of its starting date, 1873.

Macdonald came under heavy criticism in reference to these terms, on the grounds that they were too generous. An economic slump coincided with the negotiations, and this made them appear less likely to be fulfilled.

Nonetheless, by 1873 (on paper), the nation of Canada existed, stretching from the Atlantic to the Pacific. Turning the paper country into an actuality was the challenge ahead.

## 2. External
### The Treaty of Washington, 1871

Macdonald had hoped for a restoration of reciprocity between Canada and the U.S.A.; there was, however, still a significant amount of Anglo-American hostility. At the same time, the tariff had powerful supporters in Congress.

The British and the U.S.A., in 1871, decided to hold a conference to attempt to settle some of the outstanding issues between the two countries. Macdonald attended as a member of the British delegation.

Many of the differences, such as the settlement for damages caused by the *Alabama*, did not concern Canada. There was, however, a counter-claim for damage caused by the Fenian raids, the boundary between Canada and the U.S.A. off Vancouver Island was in dispute, and there was the perennial problem of U.S. fishing rights in the coastal waters of the Maritimes.

Macdonald, unfortunately, was unable to persuade the British to take a hard line on any of the Canadian problems. So far as the imperial government was concerned, the object of the conference was to ease difficulties, not cause them. Canada's claims would have to take second place to the larger aim of Anglo-American friendship. In the event, some sacrifices were made by Canada to this end.

Through the Treaty of Washington (1871), the British were to settle the Fenian claims themselves. The boundary off Vancouver island (and the *Alabama* claims) went to international arbitration. U.S. fishermen were to be allowed to enter Canadian coastal waters, the price for this privilege similarly to be reached by arbitration.

The Treaty was unpopular in Canada, on the grounds that Macdonald had permitted U.S. entry to the inshore fishing grounds, but had been unable to obtain reciprocity.

## 3. Downfall of the Macdonald Administration

Macdonald's downfall was caused by a combination of the economic crisis of the early 1870's, the unfavorable reaction to the terms for the entry of British Columbia to Confederation, the cool reception to the Treaty of Washington and the Pacific Scandal.

The Pacific Scandal arose out of matters concerning the railway to be built to British Columbia in accordance with the terms of entry of that colony into Confederation. At first, the federal government decided that the project could best be handled by private enterprise with some government support in the form of land.

Two companies tried for the contract. One consisted almost entirely of men from Ontario. The other had the support of U.S. capital and was organized by a Montreal financier, Sir Hugh Allan. Macdonald was inclined to the latter group, but demanded that Allan purge the U.S. group from the company. Not only did Allan do this, but he also made a considerable donation to Conservative party funds (for the election of 1872).

Shortly after Macdonald's re-election in 1872, the railway contract was formally handed to Allan's company. Then the opposition Liberal party discovered the details of the campaign donation. Macdonald's own followers found it difficult to accept his denial that the donation had had anything to do with the award of the contract. As a result, Macdonald left office in November, 1873, and an election followed.

## XII. The Liberal Administration, 1873-1878

The Liberals enjoyed their strongest support in Ontario. The Prime Minister was Alexander Mackenzie, a stonemason from Sarnia. Mackenzie was an organizer and administrator rather than a leader, and lacked the spark of imagination.

### 1. The Clerical Problem
#### a. Background

The Liberal party was extremely unpopular with the Catholic hierarchy in Quebec. This was largely because of a confusion of names; the bishops assumed that the Liberals of Ontario were identical with the liberals of Europe, who were usually connected with revolution and radical reform.

Opposition to the Liberals was centered around a group of leading priests, who were linked with a powerful European group which held that any Catholic's prime duty was to the Pope "over the mountains". This group became known as the Ultramontane Party. The Canadian leader during this period was the Bishop of Montreal, Monseigneur Bourget.

Bourget took the Liberal party to be an anti-clerical group. Another organization which he suspected of this trait was the Institut Canadien in Montreal. This was really a library and discussion center founded in 1844. In some discussions, no doubt, radical doctrines were put forward, and the bishop took these to be typical of the proceedings and aims of the Institut.

In addition, it had numbered among its members such men as Papineau, who had been anti-clerical to the extent that he insisted the church should remain out of secular activity. Further, the library of the Institut included books on the Catholic Index.

When Bourget demanded the removal of the forbidden books, the Institut took the attitude that this was a secular matter over which he had no authority. The dispute went on for years. At last, in 1869, Bourget issued a notice to the effect that Catholics might not be members of the Institut. Offenders were to be denied the sacraments. He obtained the support of the Pope for the pastoral letter containing the decree.

Soon afterwards, Joseph Guibord, a Catholic member of the Institut, died. Bourget denied his family the right of burying him in holy ground. Other Institut members persuaded the family to take the case to court.

### b. During the Liberal Administration

Soon after the Liberals came to power, the Judicial Committee of the (British) Privy Council — at that time the final court of appeal for Canadians — handed down a decision that the family had a right to bury the body in a Catholic churchyard.

The first attempt at a funeral provoked a near-riot; at the second attempt the army kept order. On the following day, the bishop deconsecrated the ground in which the body was buried.

This episode exemplifies the attitude of some of the Catholic higher clergy towards anti-clerical organizations. At that point, a young Quebec Liberal, Wilfrid Laurier, decided to attempt to dispel the belief of the church that Canadian liberalism was anticlerical and revolutionary.

In 1877, in a speech entitled *Political Liberalism*, he contradicted the bishop's arguments. He attempted to show that the Catholic Church, as an organization, was not a target of the Liberal party. On the other hand, he came out unequivocally against clerical influence upon Catholics in political matters.

However, Laurier did not wish to see a Catholic party formed, to enter politics. He was, therefore relieved when the Pope of the time (Leo XIII) declared that priests in Canada ought not to interfere in politics at any level. At the same time, the Pope made it clear that he differentiated between the Canadian Liberal party and European liberalism. As a result, Quebec priests were no longer permitted to suggest to their charges that it was sinful to vote in any particular way in an election.

## 2. Reforms
   a. The secret ballot was introduced during this administration.

b. Election expenses were to be controlled by law.

c. Bribery of civil servants was made a serious offence by the Corrupt Practices Act.

d. The Governor-General's independence in procedure with the advice of the Cabinet was made clearer and restricted.

e. The Canadian Supreme Court, established by the British North America Act (1867), was organized in 1875. This had the effect of cutting down the amount of appeals referred to the Judicial Committee of the (British) Privy Council. It served as a further example of Canada's growing nationhood.

The Minister of Justice, Edward Blake, was closely connected with the political reforms of this administration.

## 3. The Economy
a. The intercontinental railway ran into more difficulties. The heavy financial burden was necessarily borne by the East which complained of the cost, while the middle and far West complained about the slow progress. It was clear that financial and physical difficulties had been under-estimated.

b. The Mackenzie government tried to succeed where Macdonald had failed, in negotiating a fresh reciprocity treaty with the U.S.A. It was no more successful than he had been.

c. The intercolonial railway was one bright spot, for it was finally completed in 1876.

## 4. The Election of 1878
This election campaign saw the inauguration of the "National Policy" plank in the Conservative platform. Generally, this was a policy composed of general economic expansion, encouragement of immigration, federal aid to railway building, and, basically, the protective tariff.

This, together with the leadership of Sir John A. Macdonald and electoral disaffection with the Liberal record, ensured the election of a Conservative administration.

# XIII. The Conservatives in Power, 1878-1896

## 1. The National Policy
a. The intercontinental railway was pushed on by means of Macdonald's original policy of private building with federal assistance. A

new company was formed, controlled by Donald Smith of the Hudson's Bay Company and George Stephen of the Bank of Montreal.

To this group, the federal government offered that part of the Canadian Pacific Railway already completed (700 miles), permanent tax relief, an embargo on competitive lines to the south for twenty years, tax-free import of construction materials, $25 million in cash and 25,000,000 acres of good western land.

In return the railway was to be completed by 1891. However, by 1883 the syndicate was asking for a further federal subsidy almost as large as the original. This was granted. Two years later, another request was made, and met. (Between the two last requests, the C.P.R. had demonstrated its strategic worth by being used to send out troops for the Second Riel Rebellion, see below.)

Macdonald's insistence on the completion of the intercontinental railroad was finally rewarded in 1885 when the two lines, one from the Pacific and the other from the East, were linked.

b. Unfortunately, the immigration policy was not as successful as the railway policy. There was an international economic slump and migration was unattractive. There was little economic expansion to attract settlers, because the depression had dried up sources of capital for new enterprise. At the same time, little outside capital was available.

By 1891, deaths and emigration to the U.S.A. exceeded Canadian births. Both the population and the economy stagnated.

c. The tariff was increased in 1879, on a wide list of both manufactured and agricultural goods coming into the country. The highest duties were on manufactured goods, so that Canadian industry was protected. This feature of the National Policy has been generally maintained since 1879, and few administrations have made any notable attempts to alter the system of tariffs.

d. Generally the hopes and promises of the National Policy were not attained during this government's period in office.

## 2. Sectional and Cultural Problems

a. In the Middle West, economic problems prevailed. The settlers blamed the National Policy and the federal government. In particular, they resented the tariff as a device to raise the price for goods they needed from the East.

They also attacked the Canadian Pacific Railway's monopoly and complained of its high freight rates. As the administration stayed in office, there was a growing western attitude that the federal government was not interested in Manitoban economic problems. There was some talk of an uprising and the Manitoba Farmers Union was organized with a program of direct action.

b. A more serious and urgent problem was the return of Louis

Riel. This time, he was connected with both Métis and Indian discontent. Many Indians suffered from starvation, numerous deaths by smallpox, and the dishonest or incompetent administration of reservations. The Métis had new grounds for resentment. A proportion of the Métis had gone to the Northwest after the first Riel Rebellion. Towards the mid-1880's eastern settlers and immigrants began to penetrate the area. Complaints from the Métis that they were being cheated of their land received little or no attention in Ottawa. In fact, the federal government failed to realize, throughout, the growing seriousness of the situation. Métis' requests for legal recognition of their land claims were ignored.

Riel reached Prince Albert in 1885. At once the Métis were joined by many Indian tribes. The first fighting occurred at Duck Lake in March of the same year. The federal government then sent a force whose rapid transit was made possible by the new inter-continental railroad.

Within two months Riel was defeated and forced to surrender. English Canada demanded that he be tried for treason and the death of Thomas Scott fifteen years earlier. Once again, however, Quebec saw him as a fellow-defender of the rights of a minority group, even though a group of French-Canadian troops had been sent west to defeat him.

Riel was tried later the same year and accused of being a madman. He was found guilty after insisting he was sane. Macdonald did not exercise his prerogative of reprieve and Riel was executed. At once, he became a martyr insofar as the French Canadian minority was concerned. As a result, ethnic differences in the country as a whole were aggravated. The resulting discontent wrecked Macdonald's own party and administration.

c. In Quebec, the Conservatives lost ground rapidly after the execution of Riel and Macdonald's defamatory remarks. The incident had served to remind French Canadians that they were a minority and that their interests would not be served, in a simple choice, if they were opposed to those of the rest of the country.

Although the French-Canadian members of Macdonald's cabinet remained loyal to the party, in the provincial election a united Liberal and French Canadian nationalist group swept the Conservatives from office. The new provincial leader was Mercier. (Despite this, the federal Conservative party was returned to power in the election of 1887).

d. Federal-provincial relations also developed added problems during this administration. Macdonald's conceptions of the federal system were under fire in both Manitoba and Ontario. In particular, his central premise of a strong federal government able to disallow provincial legislation was unpopular in Manitoba.

The reason was that the provincial government had attempted to by-pass the Canadian Pacific Railway, which was under Macdonald's protection, by chartering competitive railways south to the U.S.A. Macdonald had vetoed the legislation. As a result, there was widespread disaffection on the Prairies.

The cause of similar discontent in Ontario was the veto by Macdonald of provincial laws concerned with inland navigation. In the Maritimes, however, economic problems were blamed on the federal government. The principal culprit, it was thought, was the tariff. Feeling was so strong that in 1886 the Nova Scotia assembly put through a motion insisting that the province had a right to secede at will.

By 1887, provincial discontent was so great that Ontario and Quebec sponsored an interprovincial conference. Only the Conservative legislatures of Prince Edward Island and British Columbia failed to send a delegation. The conference was ignored by Macdonald.

The meeting demanded increased federal financial aid, the repeal of the right of disallowance by the federal government, the power to pass matters to the British government, and a demand for a provincial say in the selection of federal senators.

Macdonald's attitude of ignoring this provincial opposition was weakened when the lesser governments persisted in appealing unpopular decisions to the Judicial Committee of the Privy Council in London. By 1885, it became clear that the interpretation of this body was increasingly to narrow the powers of the federal government and widen those of the provincial bodies. By 1895, by constant appeal to Britain, the provinces had much more legislative power than had been anticipated in 1867.

## 3. The Election of 1891

In the decade after the execution of Riel, relations between English and French Canada deteriorated, and then became critical. The economic depression failed to yield to any counter-measures. The National Policy was consonant with failure. The high tariff, associated with Macdonald and the Conservatives, was taken to be the greatest single cause of the slump in Canada.

Western farmers and the Maritimes began to demand reciprocity with the U.S.A. The Liberal party took this up as part of its campaign platform. When the election of 1891 arrived, the principal choice was between the National Policy and unrestricted reciprocity.

The Liberal case was that the cancellation of all duties between Canada and the U.S.A. would end the slump on the North American continent. They advocated that each country, however, should maintain its tariffs against the rest of the world.

Macdonald's counter-argument was that this was not feasible, unless Canada had exactly the same tariff as the U.S.A. with reference to the rest of the world, which clearly cut out imperial preferences. He also feared that a joint tariff might well lead to some form of economic union between the two countries; he felt that political union would be bound to follow any such arrangement.

He was not against reaching some form of trade agreement with the U.S.A., and in 1891 he tried, but failed, to negotiate an economic treaty with that country.

In the election campaign, the Conservative platform was "the old man, the old flag, the old policy", an appeal to tradition and sentiment which just, but only just, secured a personal victory for Sir John. In the last resort, it had been the business element, who needed the high tariff, which had enabled the Conservatives to limp to victory.

Macdonald died shortly after the election, leaving the Conservatives leaderless.

## 4. The Final Conservative Administration, 1891-1896
### a. Sectional Problems

Relations between French Canada and the rest of the country were marked by increased resentment. The French Canadians began to withdraw into a nationalistic posture, on guard against any attack on their identity.

At the same time, English Canada was increasingly insensitive to the expansion of French Canadian culture outside Quebec. The demands for minority rights by French Canadian groups outside that province were generally ignored.

The problem was exaggerated when the Quebec legislature passed the Jesuit Estates Act in 1888. (The Society of Jesus had been temporarily abolished over a century before. Its possessions in the colony of Canada had become Crown property. The Society had been restored by the Pope in 1842; there was then a reasonable demand for the return of its Canadian estates.)

By the Act, the Quebec legislature valued the lost estates at $400,000. All but $60,000 was to be handed over to the Catholic Church to be allocated as the Pope saw fit. The $60,000 was to go to Protestant schools.

The Act aroused great resentment in Ontario. There was a demand for the exercise of disallowance. Macdonald declined. His action caused a Conservative party split. Thirteen Conservative M.P.'s (the "Noble Thirteen", or the "Devil's Dozen"), broke openly with Macdonald in the vote for disallowance. The most prominent anti-Catholic and francophobe was D'Alton McCarthy, who then began a campaign to end the official use of French and separate schools in provinces outside Quebec.

As a result of his activities, in 1890 Manitoba had abolished French as an official language and all but ended separate schools.

These had been officially assured in the 1870 Manitoba Act, but now the provincial government cancelled the allocation of public funds for this purpose.

As this question went through the legal process of appeal, it caused the splintering of the Conservative party. Absence of firm leadership hastened this. Macdonald had three apparent successors — Sir Charles Tupper, Sir Hector Langevin and Sir John Thompson. Tupper preferred to remain in Britain as Commissioner. Langevin was about to commit political suicide in a scandal. Thompson had himself been converted to Catholicism.

Sir John Abbott became Prime Minister, but soon resigned. Thompson succeeded him, but died after two years. These changes in leadership occurred while the Manitoba Schools Question was splitting the country. Finally old Mackenzie Bowell became the party leader. He proved to be ineffective.

In 1892, it was decided that Manitoba had been entitled to take the action which had abolished separate schools. The problem now was, could the federal government take action under Section 93 of the British North America Act (1867)?

This section specified that the federal government could be appealed to by a minority which felt that its educational and language rights, *which it possessed at the time of confederation*, were endangered.

This problem was eventually taken to the Judicial Committee of the (British) Privy Council, which held that the federal government could intervene in Manitoba. The Conservative administration, however, took no decisive action despite this ruling. In early 1896, seven cabinet members went so far as to resign in protest, but were persuaded to return.

In February, 1896, the administration brought in a bill to require the Manitoba provincial legislature to allow separate schools to be restored. The opposition in the federal parliament therupon started a filibuster. After four weeks of fruitless debate, the Conservatives allowed the bill to be talked out.

Shortly afterwards, the Commons was dissolved and an election called.

## b. The Election of 1896

As the campaign began, Bowell resigned, and Tupper returned from Britain to fight the election as Conservative leader. It was, however, a party with an internal cleavage which entered the race. It was hoped that the recent attempted legislation in favor of the Manitoban Catholics would pay dividends with the Quebec Catholics and thus restore the balance of the lost English Canadian support.

This was, generally, not the case. The Catholic hierarchy of the province, with a fine disregard to the Pope's directive after the Joseph Guibord case, gave the Conservatives firm and public support. A statement of policy or *mandement* was issued by the bishops which put the seal of approval on the Conservative entries.

On the other hand, Protestant groups were equally involved in their support of the opposition candidates and their resistance to the remedial bill for Manitoba. It was clear that a religious split had aggravated the political and ethnic cleavage in the country.

The leader of the Liberals was the French Canadian, Laurier. He had taken power in the party in 1887. Although he had opposed the remedial bill, he was entirely in favor of separate schools. His entire approach to all problems was based on friendly and reasonable negotiation. Generally speaking, he had made an excellent impression and continued to gain support in English Canada.

In the event, he was elected with a clear majority. The Quebec electorate, protected by the secret ballot, resisted the advice of their priests and voted against the Conservatives. At the same time, Laurier split the Province of Ontario, and this proved to be the crucial fact of the election.

## XIV. The Laurier Ministry, 1896-1911

Laurier began by at once persuading the provincial government in Manitoba to make some concessions to the French Canadians there. The result was a compromise which temporarily ended the crisis, but really satisfied no one permanently.

Laurier was aware that his basic problem was to solve the ethnic and sectional problems which were destroying the country. He never lost sight of the fact that he was attempting to cultivate a common national image, which would be wide enough to win the favor of all the groups forming Canada.

To this end, he selected a cabinet which has become known as "the government of all the talents." This included Fielding of Nova Scotia (Finance), Sifton of Manitoba (Interior), Tarte of Quebec (Public Works), and Mowat of Ontario (Justice).

### 1. The Economy

Laurier's theories of national economic expansion were really very similar to those of Macdonald. He also had the good fortune to be elected at a time when international prosperity was returning.

He began by introducing the so-called Fielding tariff in 1897. Although the Liberals as a party had always taken up a position for free trade and had come out often enough for reciprocity, Fielding was convinced that protection was needed at the time.

The system was changed, though, in that Canada offered to reduce tariffs against any country which would reciprocate in reference to Canada. This was really an appeal to Britain, which was Canada's most important market and source at the time. None the less, the tariff was clearly designed to protect Canadian industry and agriculture.

The tariff was, in fact, only slightly altered throughout the entire Liberal administration. It would probably have been made even more protectionist if the Liberals could have resisted pressure from the western farmers against any tariff at all.

## 2. Immigration

This was the concern of Sir Clifford Sifton, who pursued the task of settling the Prairies vigorously. Again, he was aided by the return of world prosperity: In addition, there were local reasons for the western boom (see below).

Transportation companies were brought into the immigration program, but the initiative remained always with the federal government and the Ministry of the Interior. It set up the North Atlantic Trading Agency, a cover organization for passing out information about Canada in Europe, and organizing the flow of immigrants from there to Canada.

Sifton's own attitude was that Canada needed farmers rather than urban dwellers and workers, and the emphasis was in attracting and moving the Central European farmer. Actually, the peak year for immigration was 1913, after the Liberal administration had left office. The total that year was 400,000, but it is clear that the impetus had come from Sifton's previous work. The total in the 15 years of the Liberal administration was some 2 ¼ million — about 1 million immigrants from the British Isles, 750,000 from the U.S.A. and the rest from continental Europe.

## 3. The Western Boom

The causes of the rapid expansion of the Prairies were as follows:

a. World economic prosperity caused a renewed interest in capital investment, economic expansion and immigration. The Canadian West "existed" in time for this expansionary cycle.

b. The boom was primarily based on wheat, for which the Prairies had ideal soil and climate. Developments made the area even more suitable once the industry was established.

c. The frontier had closed in the U.S.A. There had been, since 1893, no more good free land for the sod-busters. The last frontier in North America lay in the Canadian West.

d. There was a change in the migratory pattern of Canadians, who began to move to their own west rather than to the U.S.A.

e. There was massive immigration from the U.S.A. and Europe (see above).

f. The growing population in Europe, especially urban population, caused a demand for wheat. Canada was the only new source of grain for this new market.

g. At the same time, urban development in the traditional market, the U.S.A., plus the complicating factors of that country's own increased population, industrialization and lack of expansion capability in grain farming, meant that it could not compete for the new markets.

h. Naturally, the increasing shortages caused by the last two factors tended to push up the price of wheat, making grain farming a more attractive prospect.

i. There was an improvement in the design, speed and capacity of bulk grain carriers on the Atlantic run. As a result, freight rates fell rapidly during this period. At the same time, internal freight rates were set up by the federal government.

j. A new type of rapidly-maturing wheat was developed by the Canadian, Charles Marquis. This strain needed fewer frost-free days to reach maturity. As a result, it could be grown further north, so that greater areas in Canada now became available for wheat growing.

k. In the same way, dryland wheat farming had reached its highest perfection on the U.S. prairies. These methods were not only copied, but their proponents immigrated into Canada from the northern U.S. states to carry on wheat farming.

The western boom gave an immense impetus to the entire national economy. Service industries grew up on the Prairies and basic industry expanded in the eastern provinces, especially Ontario. There was railroad expansion (see below), together with economic activity in practically every field (see Trade and Industry, below).

## 4. Constitutional Problems in the New West

In 1905, the Laurier administration carved the two provinces of Alberta and Saskatchewan out of the southern part of the Northwest Territories. Problems arose at once about language and education in the new provinces.

The new provinces were set up by autonomy bills, drawn up by Laurier. These included a section which brought back the school organization as it had existed before 1875 in the Territories. There was a storm of protest in English Canada, which reached into the cabinet itself. Sifton resigned. As a result, Laurier was forced to withdraw this clause and leave the western school system as it was running when the new provinces were set up.

## 5. The Railways

The Canadian Pacific Railway proved insufficient to meet the requirements of the expansion and soon there were demands for an extended railway system on the Prairies. In 1902, the Grand Trunk Railway decided to commit itself to an intercontinental line and asked for federal financial assistance. At the same time, a second group, led by Donald Mann and William Mackenzie, put forward plans for a third intercontinental line, the Canadian Northern. The authorities attempted to persuade the two groups to merge, but unsuccessfully. Laurier finally allowed both companies to go forward with their plans, with generous government subsidies.

The two intercontinental systems were completed. By the time they were fully operational, the rapid expansion of the West had ceased, and existing facilities were ample for the stable economy. As with the Canadian Pacific Railway a generation earlier, the costs of construction and operation had been underestimated. The lines were not well run when completed, and there was some corruption in the handling of contracts.

When completed, the two systems were in competition in areas which would scarcely support one line. The railway expansion was one aspect of the western boom and the Laurier administration which came near to being a complete failure. (In 1923, the federal government found it necessary to take over the two new railroads and run them at a loss as a nationalized corporation, Canadian National Railways.)

## 6. Trade and Industry

Trade and industry expanded considerably during the period. The progress was in widely diversified areas, and was not restricted to wheat and agriculture. Wheat itself, of course, made a tremendous contribution. Wheat exports between 1891 and 1910 rose by 7500 per cent. However, manufacturing and the export trade showed equally significant increases.

Perhaps the most exciting development was the discovery of gold in the Klondike, in the Yukon Territory. This field was at its most active from 1898-1903, though it still produces limited amounts of ore.

In British Columbia, Quebec and Ontario, there were great increases in the lumber and pulp industries. In Ontario and British Columbia there were significant developments in the mining and metal industries. In the former, there was a mining boom around Sudbury, while in the latter there were such features as the largest smelter in the British Empire at Trail.

In Ontario, the expansion in trade combined with a demand for power brought about the organization of the Ontario Hydro-Electric Commission and the building of the tremendous power complex at Niagara. The flood of immigrants, the expansion of industry and the opening of the Prairies caused a construction boom, particularly in Ontario and along the Canadian Pacific Railway line on the Prairies.

There were, of course, resulting problems. Big business arrived in the form of monopolies and giant corporations. Existing laws proved incapable of dealing with the worse abuses of these organizations. New legislation, such as the Combines Investigation Act (1910), were insufficient to curb the dangers.

The industrial working class increasingly organized itself in defence of its interests. The groundwork had been laid with the organization of the Trades and Labour Congress of Canada (1886), which expanded rapidly during the boom. The majority of union effort was expended to obtain the right of collective bargaining. The unions lacked strength in the last resort, however, and when disputes came down to strikes the employees usually lost.

The Crow's Nest Pass Agreement (1897) was a partial answer to the demands of organized agriculture on the Prairies. The Canadian Pacific Railway was engaged in the expensive task of driving a new route through the Rockies via Crow's Nest Pass. The federal government agreed to subsidize this activity; in return, the railway was required to carry agricultural produce and machinery at fixed and reduced rates. There was also a western demand for a railway to Churchill, Manitoba, a summer port on Hudson Bay, which, it was believed, would reduce freight rates to the European market. (This was eventually completed in 1931.)

## 7. Reciprocity and the Tariff, 1910-1911

By 1910, there was a demand from the western farmer for the reduction of the tariff which could no longer be ignored. Influential groups such as the Farmers' Association in Ontario, agricultural newspapers, and the Grain Growers' Associations were united in their clamor for revision.

At the same time, they demanded the return of reciprocity with the U.S.A. and an increased British Empire preference. By coincidence, there was a revival of interest in reciprocity in the U.S.A. at the same time. Laurier became involved in negotiations with them, and in early 1911 emerged with an agreement which allowed reciprocity on a wide list of natural resources, and reduced the tariffs on many manufactured goods.

Unfortunately, Laurier had not taken into account all the circumstances involved in a treaty of this nature. Important mercantile organizations were utterly opposed to any reduction of the tariff behind which their businesses operated. Nor was party any criterion as to the attitude towards the agreement. The disaffected Sifton led a Toronto group which came out as being completely opposed to Laurier's policy.

The agreement rapidly became a divisive issue. An election was to be fought in 1911, and reciprocity was one of the basic issues on which it was fought. (See Election of 1911, below.)

## 8. Imperial Affairs

Laurier's aim, so far as imperial affairs were concerned, was to make Canada a strong autonomous country inside the Empire organization. In this, too, he ran into problems which were to affect the election of 1911.

The situation, when Laurier took office, was that Canada had no diplomatic relations with any country. Britain looked after this aspect of Canadian affairs. However, there had been a Canadian High Commissioner in London since 1880, and the Conservatives had obtained the right to deal with foreign countries on trade matters. There had been a precedent for independent military action when Macdonald had refused to send a detachment to the Sudan in one of Britain's colonial wars (1885).

Laurier's attitude was somewhat the same, but the problems he faced were more pressing and difficult. There had sprung up in the home country a group which put forward the concept of imperial unity, with an imperial parliament, imperial forces and a common imperial foreign and defence policy. Laurier, of course, was entirely opposed to all of these.

The chief proponent of these ideas in Britain was Joseph Chamberlain, and they took on a new importance when he was made Colonial Secretary (1895). He at once set about trying to organize the Empire into a world-wide confederation ruled from London. As such, he was bound to meet Laurier head on.

Most French Canadians and many English Canadians were also completely opposed to imperial federation, but there was a significant group of English Canadians who were entirely in favor. As a result, Laurier was forced to compromise, a course which eventually satisfied no one.

In 1897, Laurier went to the first imperial conference in London. At this, Chamberlain intended to put forward his plans for a tighter imperial organization. Laurier completely refused to consider Chamberlain's plan for a permanent imperial council. His attitude was that colonies naturally developed into autonomous nations, and that such a council would be incongruous.

He insisted that any Canadian commitment to the Empire, such as imperial preferences, must remain entirely voluntary. He was soon to have a more difficult matter than trade to deal with.

The Boer War broke out in 1899. It caused a wave of imperial fervor in the English Canadian sections of the established parts of Canada. In Britain, Chamberlain used the War to further promote imperial federation and unity. He put forward the idea that Canadian troops should be sent to South Africa as a gesture of Empire solidarity. English Canadians were heartily in favor of this, while French Canadians were completely opposed.

As a compromise, Laurier agreed to have equipped and trained one battalion of imperial volunteers. On arrival in South Africa, the British would be responsible for the group. He made it clear that this was an isolated instance and not to be regarded as a habit or precedent. (In the event, 7,000 men actually went from Canada, some as volunteers in the British Army.)

During the public debate on this matter, the Conservatives raised the predictable charge that Laurier was a traitor and an enemy of the British Empire. On the other hand, French Canadians portrayed him as a traitor to his heritage and as imperialist as any Conservative Englishman.

His heir-apparent in Quebec, Henri Bourassa, publicly broke with Laurier and resigned from the federal parliament. However, most Canadians accepted Laurier's decision as the most reasonable possible in the circumstances.

In 1902, at the next imperial conference, he again made it clear that he was not prepared to give Britain a blank cheque as regards military commitment of Canadian forces in Britain's wars, at the same time maintaining his attitude that Canada could not accept any form of political direction from London, except voluntarily.

This remained the state of affairs until the eruption of the Canadian Navy question in the closing years of the administration. As the arms race between Britain and Germany increased in intensity towards 1910, Britain began to look to the Empire for help in imperial defence. The grounds were that it ought not to be the responsibility of the Briton to pay for the entire defence of the Empire.

Laurier's attitude was that Canada's best help would be to develop its own forces and defences; as such, he refused to make any peacetime military commitment. Further, he wished Canadian forces to be under Canadian command, and the last British commander (and British units) left Canada during this period.

But demands mounted, both in Canada and Britain, for more concrete evidence, and this finally took the form of pressure for the inauguration of a Canadian Navy. At last, in 1910, Laurier committed himself to a small, completely Canadian, fleet.

There was opposition from all sides. The nationalist French Canadian group, now led by Bourassa, condemned Laurier as having committed Canada to Britain's wars. The English Conservatives claimed that any Canadian Navy would be bound to be second-rate and that the better contribution would have been money to help run the Royal Navy.

After a long parliamentary wrangle, the Navy Bill passed into law in late 1910, but the issue was by no means dead, and formed one of the main issues of the 1911 election.

Britain donated to Canada two old cruisers in 1911 to train a navy. The Canadian Navy then became a political issue again, so that by the outbreak of war the Royal Canadian Navy consisted solely of these two vessels.

## 9. U.S. - Canadian Relations

Apart from the reciprocity negotiations (see above), the principal dealings between Canada and the U.S.A. were connected with the Alaskan Panhandle Dispute.

The Anglo-Russian Treaty of 1825 had given the Russians a continuous strip of coast thirty miles wide south from Alaska. The wording of the Treaty with reference to the actual drawing of the boundary was so loose that one possible interpretation would place the inland stretches of some of the longer fjords in Canadian territory. Alaska, of course, had become U.S. territory in 1867.

The Klondike gold rush served to bring the area into prominence and the dispute to a head. Both countries wanted one fjord, the Lynn Canal, which gave good access to the new goldfields.

Canada wished to have the case referred to an international body for arbitration. The ebullient Theodore Roosevelt was not prepared to negotiate at all on these grounds, but was willing to submit the matter to a judicial body, one-half the members of which would be Americans.

Canada, with misgivings, agreed and nominated two justices to a six-man commission. Britain supplied the sixth, Lord Alverstone.

Before the commission met (1903), the U.S. President gave notice that he had no intention of accepting a decision adverse to the U.S. claim. His three representatives had been chosen on the basis of their certainty to approve the American position.

In the event, the U.S. had the better claim, but it fell to the British representative to be the only judge not to make his decision follow national lines. He had had the difficult task of being impartial and of not harming Anglo-American relations. Therefore, practically all the American case was accepted.

Violent protest followed in Canada, not so much against the decision as against the British judge. The Canadian Prime Minister observed publicly that Canada might well begin to look after her own external affairs. The ultimate result, however, was a worsening of the anti-American feeling in Canada, and this played an important part in the election of 1911.

## 10. The Election of 1911

The election of 1911 was fought on three main issues. These were reciprocity, imperial federation and the navy issue. As a result, it was confused and filled with shifting loyalties.

People who did not want reciprocity claimed that Laurier was handing Canada over to the U.S. A prominent group in his own party announced that it was withdrawing its support.

In Quebec, a coalition of the Conservatives and the group led by Henri Bourassa campaigned against Laurier. Bourassa argued that Laurier was a tool of imperialism, while the Conservatives denounced him as not having his heart in the British Empire.

This unlikely coalition, led by Sir Robert Borden, proved to be the winner. Unfortunately, since victory had been gained as a coalition, it was to prove difficult to organize a policy which would suit all the groups who had contributed to the victory.

# XV. The Conservative Administration, 1911-1917

## 1. Inherited Problems

Borden had the perennial problem of trying to maintain some form of unity between English and French Canadians. In the economic field he was faced with the shift from world prosperity to depression, together with the end of the great years of the western boom. There was a drying-up of foreign risk capital, world grain prices went down and unemployment became a pressing problem.

His first political problem, however, was the navy. A visit to Britain soon after election assured him that world war was imminent and that some action would have to be taken to help Britain with the burden of imperial defence.

His suggestion was to send 35 million dollars to Britain, as a gift to be used in the construction of the most recent naval weapon, the dreadnought. On the other hand, like Laurier, he made it clear that this was to be no precedent; the aim was for Canada to have a say in the policy which might result in the warships being committed to action.

Borden's bill went through the Commons, but unfortunately, the Senate retained a Liberal majority after fifteen years of Liberal administrations. The upper house rejected the bill. When war did occur, Canada neither had a navy, beyond two old British training vessels, nor had contributed to imperial defence in cash.

## 2. Canada and World War I

The status of Canada in 1914 was such that Britain's declaration of war automatically involved Canada in the conflict. At the outset, there was some feeling of common aim towards victory. As the War went on, this gradually diminished.

## a. Military Affairs

Canada began by passing the War Measures Act (1914), which gave the administration wide scope in governing without the confines of parliamentary procedure. The first military commitment was to raise and train a force of 25,000. Before Christmas, 1914, Canadian troops were disembarking in Europe.

In 1915, Canadian troops were organized into the Canadian Corps. When the War ended in 1918, the army enlistments had totalled over 600,000. Over one-quarter of the pilots in the Royal Air Force had been Canadians, while the navy had taken responsibility for guarding the eastern coast.

On the Western Front, in 1915, Canadian forces had held off the first gas attack (at Ypres). On the Somme, the Canadians were constantly in action and it was here that most of the casualties were suffered in the debilitating trench warfare.

The major Canadian engagement, and the most expensive in terms of lives, was the storming of Vimy Ridge in 1917, under the command of a pre-war Canadian militiaman, General Sir Arthur Currie. The total casualties of Canadian forces during the War exceeded 60,000 killed (more than the U.S.A.).

## b. War Economy

There was a growing European demand for Canadian grain, so that the western boom was revived and extended. Prices escalated, so that by 1917 the federal government was forced to resort to compulsory adjustment. This was done by the organization of a Board of Grain Supervisors.

Another natural resource which experienced a growing demand was forest products, but all fields of industry were stimulated to some degree. One result was that Canadian heavy industry expanded rapidly. The Imperial Munitions Board was organized to direct arms production. It can reasonably be said that the main economic result of World War I was to change Canada from a basically agricultural country into an industrial nation.

In the field of finance, the War practically ended European investment. Canada was increasingly forced to look inwards for capital. As a result, in 1917, federal income tax was introduced.

There were the usual wartime phenomena of shortages, rising prices and inflation. There was an attempt to combat these at the federal level by the organization of such offices as the Food Controller, the War Trade Board, and the Cost of Living Commissioners. These measures were easily evaded and not particularly effective; the result was resentment which was to be an unpleasant legacy after the war.

## c. The Conscription Crisis of 1917

By mid-1917, enough reinforcements could not be found by voluntary enlistment to keep the Canadian Army up to desired strength. The government had earlier promised not to introduce conscription. It now proposed to go back on this undertaking.

In 1914, it had not appeared that compulsory military service would be necessary for victory. French Canada was completely opposed to it, with Bourassa as its spokesman. There was less feeling of involvement in the European conflict in Quebec. In addition, there was widespread opposition to conscription among industrial workers and in rural areas throughout Canada.

French Canada was still largely agricultural and the young men tended to remain on the farm and, at the same time, marry younger. Similar feelings motivated opposition to conscription in other areas of Canada. Voluntary enlistment in Quebec was handled in an uninspired way; training was in English, French Canadian drafts were split up into English-speaking units, and at one stage the entire recruiting in Quebec was under authority of a Protestant clergyman.

As a result, recruiting in French Canada was much below that of the rest of the country. The Minister of Militia, Sam Hughes, was a francophobe and anti-Catholic, which was scarcely an incentive to French Canadian enlistments.

In 1917, Borden visited the Western Front, and returned convinced that conscription was necessary. In an attempt to avoid an ethnic cleavage, Borden invited Laurier and the Liberals to form a coalition government with him; the responsibility for the introduction of conscription would then be shared.

Although Laurier upheld the war effort, he was completely opposed to conscription. He knew that changing his stand at that point would merely hand over political power in Quebec to the French Canadian nationalists and Bourassa. Further, he was convinced that an effort to impose conscription would actually harm the war effort by disrupting the nation.

Some Liberals, however, were prepared to enter a coalition with Borden. Sifton was one of the leaders of this group, and he began discussions with the Prime Minister. The latter, in the meantime, put two statutes through parliament which took the vote away from all immigrants from enemy countries after 1902, and enfranchised all overseas troops and their female next-of-kin in Canada.

At the election of 1917, at which compulsory militia service was the key issue, Borden obtained his mandate from this manipulated franchise. In the heat of the moment, the considerable opposition to conscription outside Quebec was ignored, and the result was interpreted as a repudiation of Quebec. In October, 1917, the Union (coalition) government took office.

**d. The Ontario Schools Dispute**

One reason for lukewarm French Canadian involvement in the "English" war was a further eruption of the separate schools problem, this time in Ontario.

In that province, a statute known as Regulation 17 restricted the teaching of French to the lower grades, and could be construed as holding back the development of complete French-language schools. Most French Canadians were more interested in the dispute over the Regulation than the War in Europe. English Canadians, however, were barely aware of the issue.

The matter went through the courts, which upheld the Ontario law. At about the same time, Manitoba terminated bilingual schools (1916). As a result, French Canadians felt that, once again, they had been the victims of discrimination.

# XVI. The Union Government, 1917-1921

## 1. Conscription

The Unionists had been almost completely successful in English Canada, but just as unsuccessful in Quebec. Laurier's fears of an ethnic split had been realized. None of the prominent French Canadian leaders held cabinet posts in the new government.

The new policy caused almost 50,000 reinforcements to be sent to the Western Front. There is no doubt, however, that the cultural split in the country was an excessive price to pay for putting these men in action. Conscription and the method by which it had been introduced left a legacy of bitterness and resentment which plagues Canada to this day.

## 2. Imperial Relations

In 1914, Canada had been at war as a result of Britain's involvement. Canada's foreign policy was directed from London. Borden was committed to move towards ending this situation. As the War continued, there was an increasing sentiment that Canada should have more control over its own interests.

Throughout the war, the Canadian government was adamant that Canadian troops should not be committed piecemeal, but should be organized as a composite Canadian force. By 1917, the Canadian Corps was commanded by a Canadian, Sir Arthur Currie.

By that time, however, the Canadian complaint was that the

British were failing to keep them fully informed about future policy, including the use of Canadian troops. There had, however, been a change of government in Britain in 1916, and a coalition government was in power, led by Liberal, David Lloyd George.

The latter accepted Borden's criticisms as reasonable, and as a result the Imperial War Cabinet was organized in 1917. This was an immense and significant step forward in Canadian autonomy. The Imperial War Cabinet consisted of all the Dominion prime ministers plus the key members of the British cabinet. Soon after the organization of this body, Borden brought forward what came to be known as Regulation IX. This called for a post-war conference to define the position of the dominions with reference to autonomy in domestic affairs, and their consultative position in foreign affairs.

Borden's concern was not limited to recognition of autonomy by Britain. He was also anxious to have Canada recognized as a nation internationally. As a result of his efforts, and despite British opposition, Canada signed the peace treaty at Versailles (1919) in her own right. The Canadian parliament ratified the treaty for Canada, not the parliament at Westminster.

Canada became a charter member of the League of Nations as an individual country. Here, Borden ran into difficulty with such countries as the U.S.A. and France, who were convinced that Canada would attend as a pocket vote for Britain.

The position in 1919, however, was that although Canada had not yet attained complete control of her external affairs, she was now by no means subordinate to Britain in this area.

## 3. Party Politics, 1919-1921

By 1919, all the old-line parties had been splintered along ethnic or sectional lines. The Unionists had coalesced to meet the wartime situation, which had now gone. The pre-war Conservative party had been an uncertain alliance with the sole motive of being against Laurier. It was time for re-organization and re-alignment of the political parties.

### a. The Liberals

Laurier died in early 1919. His heirs-apparent had become either French Canadian nationalists or Unionists. One promising Liberal, Mackenzie King, had held office as early as 1909 as Minister of Labour and had remained loyal to Laurier in 1917. As a result, he could command the support of Quebec in the future. This ensured his becoming party leader on the death of Laurier.

### b. The Conservatives

Borden retired in 1920. A conservative caucus selected Arthur Meighen to succeed him (i.e. he became Prime Minister by vote of the

Conservative M.P.'s in office, not the electorate or the party organization).

Meighen was a great debater and orator. He had been the prime advocate, in the House, of conscription. He had also been the organizer of the nationalizing of the bankrupt Grand Trunk Railway (1919).

Unfortunately for the party, Quebec found him unacceptable because of his performance on conscription, while the Prairies associated him with the unpopular high protectionist tariff.

### c. The Progressives

A farmers' political movement came to the fore immediately after the war. The leader was Thomas A. Crerar, a former Unionist who had resigned from the government at the end of the war to show his opposition to the protective tariff.

The movement resulted in the formation of the National Progressive Party in early 1920. The country's social and economic life was in a state of flux in the immediate post-war years, and it was against this background that the election of 1921 was fought.

## 4. Urban Unrest

There were many reasons for the discontent in the towns at the close of World War I. The working class had felt discriminated against in the matter of conscription during the war. Many employers and corporations, so far as the returned ex-serviceman was concerned, were in the category of war profiteers.

The trade unions were still struggling to obtain recognition of the right to collective bargaining. The cost of living had outstripped wage increases. The end of the war boom saw a trade slump, unemployment, and pay cuts for those who still had jobs.

The reaction was a series of strikes. There was the movement towards the "One Big Union" and the resulting Red Scare in North America. The epicentre of labor trouble in Canada was Winnipeg.

In May, 1919, a general strike was called in that city by its Trades and Labour Council. The aim was to show sympathy and involvement with the metalworkers' union, which had been unable to obtain the right to collective bargaining.

There was a chain reaction of smaller strikes across the country, and tension mounted. It should be remembered that this was less than two years after the Communist Revolution in Russia. The RCMP, acting on the flimsiest information, arrested several of the strike leaders, including J.S. Woodsworth.

A peaceful demonstration on June 21 was broken up by force. One man was killed. Troops appeared on the streets of the city. The strike was over, beaten. A royal commission was empowered to investigate the strike and its causes. It found that the men's complaints were generally justified and that working conditions were extremely poor. It also found that the aim of the strike was to alleviate local conditions and that there was no suggestion of a revolution.

Soon afterwards, Woodsworth, a former Methodist minister, was elected to the federal parliament, where he served for almost a generation amid universal respect.

## 5. Agrarian Discontent

Canadian farmers, outside of Quebec as well as inside, took the view that the Unionist government had broken its promises not to conscript their sons. Furthermore, they were affected as severely as the urban dweller by the post-war inflation, low incomes and high prices. They had resented the war profiteers and government scandals. There was the additional complication of the population drift from rural to urban. The tariff, of course, was a constant source of complaint.

Since 1916, the Canadian Council of Agriculture had been expounding its New National Policy, and by 1919 there was an agrarian movement at the provincial level. The policy included a lower tariff, of course, and a general demand for more direct democracy, including nationalization of transport and subsidized freight rates.

On this platform, which was the direct opposite of Macdonald's National Policy, the United Farmers of Ontario took power in that province in 1919. In 1921, a similar occurrence took place in Alberta. Manitoba was the scene of a similar takeover in 1922.

These local farmers' groups were allied with the Progressive party at the federal level.

## 6. The Election of 1921

Meighen (in power) campaigned on a platform of successful nationalization of the railways and the general wartime record of the Unionist government. On the tariff question, he was strongly in favor of retention, though the agrarian interests were completely opposed.

The Liberals, led by King, had a compromise program between the no-tariff West and the high-tariff industrial East. His aim was to avoid making enemies rather than having a concrete platform to attract friends.

Crerar saw that the tariff would be the crux of the election. He was quite opposed to it.

When the votes were counted, King had been returned with an absolute majority of a mere two seats.

# XVII. King's Liberals in Power, 1921-1930

## 1. Party Politics

King's continuing aim after the election was to obtain and retain the support of the Progressive party. The latter realized that if it did not support King, this might well mean the return of Meighen to power, and with him the higher tariff.

In any case, the Progressives were entering their decline, with cleavages within the party itself. One section was prepared to merge formally with the Liberals. An Alberta group, led by Henry Wise Wood, wanted the franchise altered to bring in occupational representation (i.e. each occupation to have M.P.'s according to the number of people engaged in that occupation), and was opposed to working with the Liberals.

With the resignation of Crerar in 1922, the Progressive party began to fall to pieces at the federal level.

## 2. The 1925 Election

By 1925, however, the immediate postwar economic problems had been alleviated. Grain prices had recovered, prosperity had returned. In particular, farmers' discontent was not as sharp. As a result, the Progressive party lost heavily in the 1925 election, retaining only two dozen seats.

Most Progressive seats went to King and the Liberals; the latter, however, lost ground in the Atlantic provinces and Ontario. The Conservatives, still led by Meighen, made gains all over the East and became the largest single group in the Commons after the election.

## 3. Constitutional Problems

The election, however, left no party with an absolute majority. King declined to resign and aspired to govern with the help of the 24 Progressives. In early 1926, a scandal erupted in the Customs Department. As a result, the Progressives withdrew their support of the Liberals.

Before a non-confidence vote could be forced in the Commons by the opposition, King requested Governor-General Lord Byng (a Briton who had commanded Canadian troops during the War), to dissolve Parliament and call a new general election.

Byng rejected the advice of the Prime Minister, pointing out that the Conservatives had a plurality in the House, and that it was less than a year since the last election.

King at once resigned. The Governor-General then invited Meighen to form an administration. Meighen, however, was obliged to depend, as King had, on the Progressives for a majority. But the Progressives had no intention of supporting him.

Within less than a week Meighen was defeated in the Commons. The Governor-General now had no choice but to allow the parties to go to the country again.

## 4. The Election of 1926

The principal point of contention of this election was the circumstance under which it had been called. King insisted that the Governor-General's action in denying him a dissolution and an election was unconstitutional and that it was a clear case of violation of Canadian autonomy in internal matters by a British representative.

Meighen, probably correctly, took the view that Byng had acted within the bounds of his office. The electorate, however, accepted the appeal to national feeling and put King in office with a substantial majority. The Progressive party disappeared as an effective force in federal politics. Meighen relinquished the leadership of the Conservatives to R.B. Bennett in 1927.

## 5. The Economy

The national economy continued to improve into the late 1920's. More important, it was increasingly diversified, both in products and in markets. In particular, it became less dependent on Britain and Europe.

Quebec and Ontario made the most progress. In these provinces, the swing from agriculture to industry continued. In other areas, however, prosperity was less well distributed. The Atlantic provinces continued to be less prosperous and continued to blame the tariff, which, they felt, was designed to assist the interior areas only.

In 1929, the economic prosperity ended abruptly, locally and internationally. The results in Canada were severe and widespread. Economic disaster in Canada followed the stock market collapse in New York in late 1929.

The worst effects were in western Canada, where economic upset coincided with climatic ravage creating havoc for homesteaders and farmers. In the East, industry stagnated; in an era of no national social security, this meant widespread urban disaster. Before long, there were 500,000 men unemployed. It was in these circumstances that the election of 1930 was fought (see below).

## 6. Canadian Foreign Policy, 1921-1930
### a. Background

With world war so recently past, there was a feeling in Canada that no policy should be followed which would increase the possibility of Canadian involvement in foreign areas. There was even a movement to reduce those commitments which Canada had already made by membership in the League of Nations. French Canada, in particular, was opposed to external involvement.

On the other hand, there was a decreasing number of people who still defended the concept of a federated British Empire with a unified foreign policy. A group of internationalists wished for stronger commitment to the League of Nations. Generally, it was the isolationist persuasion which had the most control over external policy between the two wars.

The three major influences on Canada's attitudes during the period were the geographical proximity of the U.S.A., the changing role of Canada within the British Commonwealth and, less important, Canada's international outlook as shown by her membership in the League of Nations. It was the interplay of these three factors which affected Canadian foreign policy within this period.

## b. The League of Nations

Within a very short time of its commitment to the League of Nations, the Canadian government feared that it was too stringent. In particular, Article X of the League Covenant, appeared to Canada not to be in the better interests of the country. This article called for member nations to undertake collective security against aggressors. The country's delegation to Geneva was instructed to attempt to make this article less binding.

In 1924, Canada was able to put through a motion which stated that the League would take into consideration a member's geographical location when asking for assistance against aggressors. This appeared to call for Canadian involvement only if the Americas were concerned. King's persistent attitude was that Canada supported the league, but with the strongest reservations about its powers for enforcing peace. He felt that Canada, if opposed to a common imperial foreign policy, was equally opposed to a similar policy imposed by any other international body.

## c. Canadian Autonomy in Foreign Policy

At the outset of the Liberal administration, the Empire was evolving into the British Commonwealth. The question of Canadian autonomy in the 1920's was largely concerned with an independent external policy.

At the Versailles Peace Conference in 1919, the precedent had been established of the dominions having separate representation, but meeting in advance to decide upon an agreed imperial policy. It had also been imagined that some system of "continuous consultation", as Borden had put it, would be a useful medium in deciding a joint foreign policy.

This was not King's interpretation of autonomy. Autonomy meant, he felt, absolute independence in deciding and carrying out policy; this, even if it meant a policy different to the rest of the Commonwealth. Further, he felt that such a policy should be designed to further Canadian, not Commonwealth interests. Meighen, of course, did not differentiate between Canadian and Commonwealth foreign policy, feeling that the two were bound to have the same ends.

When imperial conferences resumed in 1921, the problem of the Anglo-Japanese treaty renewal had to be faced. Britain was prepared to extend the life of this treaty because Japan had been an ally in the recent war. New Zealand and Australia were also anxious to be allied with the strongest power in the southwest Pacific.

Canada, however, was well aware that the U.S.A. felt that the treaty was aimed at itself, since the U.S.A. was the only other naval power in the Pacific. Canada felt that setting U.S. fears at rest was more important to the Commonwealth than a treaty with a foreign power, and presented this case at the conference. As a result the alliance was not renewed.

(N.B. The Imperial Conference of 1921 took place during the closing stages of the Unionist administration. Meighen, himself, presented the Canadian case at the conference. It is treated here for the sake of continuity.)

In September, 1922, the Chanak Crisis erupted. Postwar difficulties with the Turks had put a British expedition in the position of possibly having to resist the Turks by force in Chanak, a region of Asia Minor. The British asked, publicly, that Canada consider undertaking some military assistance should fighting break out.

Unfortunately, the British failed to take into account the time difference between England and Canada. King first heard of the request from his newspaper and his reaction was predictably unfavorable. His main fear was that the episode was being exaggerated in order to force an action which would later be taken as a precedent.

He insisted that he was unauthorized to act in the matter without the direction of the Canadian parliament. He also made it clear that he was not going to bring the matter before parliament. The Conservative opposition took the view that Canada ought to agree automatically to any British request for military assistance. Meighen's association with this viewpoint probably ended his prospects of an absolute majority in any future Canadian election, because the mass of the Canadian people agreed with King on this matter.

The next stage in the development of Canadian autonomy in external affairs was in the following year. In 1923, the Halibut Treaty was signed with the U.S.A. This was concerned with the perennial fishing problem; the importance of this pact was that the Canadian representative signed the treaty as the sole signatory on the Canadian side. It was the first time that a Canadian treaty had not had a British counter-signature.

At the imperial conference in the same year, it was established that all the dominions were entitled to autonomy in formulating treaties with foreign countries. At the same time, King resisted a motion that a memorandum be issued on behalf of the conference to the effect that the delegates had agreed on a basic method of arriving at foreign policy for the Commonwealth.

Again, he maintained the attitude that he was the servant of the Canadian legislature in external matters of policy. He went further, and decided that each commitment (or lack of it) to the Commonwealth would be decided by the Canadian parliament, solely with reference to the circumstances of each particular case.

The conference's acceptance of dominion autonomy in external negotiation was not issued as a statement of policy, nor was it embodied in any statute; it was, however, again stated in the formal report of the conference.

In 1925, there was further confirmation of dominion autonomy. The Locarno Treaties were negotiated in that year. They concerned only European powers, including Britain. A clause was placed in the treaties which indicated that the dominions were not implicated unless they accepted the position by signing them. (None of the dominions did sign.)

At the next imperial conference, in 1926, a definitive statement was issued on the subject of dominion status and autonomy. The 1923 conference had set up a group, chaired by Arthur Balfour, to report on the relative status of the members of the Commonwealth.

The report was made to the 1926 conference. It described the Commonwealth as a group of "autonomous communities within the British Empire, equal in status, in no way subordinate to one another in any aspect of their domestic or external affairs, though united by a common allegiance to the Crown and freely associated as members of the British Commonwealth of Nations". The importance of the report is that it described a state of affairs then in existence, not one to be aimed for.

In 1927, Canada appointed its first ambassador (to Washington). In 1929, Canada signed the Kellogg-Briand Pact — by which the U.S.A. and France promised never to go to war against each other, and invited other nations to signify abandonment of war as an instrument of policy by countersigning it — in its own right as an independent nation.

## 7. The Election of 1930

Despite the constant impingement of external and Commonwealth affairs during the King administration, the election of 1930 was fought almost entirely against the background of the economic distress caused by the advent of the depression in 1929.

The Liberal party felt that the slump was purely temporary, that the normal practice in government and commerce would bring back the flow of prosperity, and that unemployment would soon be reduced to normal levels.

The Conservatives, now led by R.B. Bennett, however, took the position that the economy had collapsed. Protective tariffs should be increased to preserve what was left of production, and the federal government should commit itself to works projects to alleviate unemployment.

Bennett also felt that an aggressive external trade policy at the federal level would revive the business system. This appeal to action, rather than resignation to waiting the turn of events, caused the Conservatives to be elected with a majority of 31 seats.

# XVIII. Bennett's Conservatives in Power, 1930-1935

## 1. Economic Problems

Bennett recalled Parliament at once. In a special session, legislation was put through organizing a public works program, raising the tariff and allocating more funds for federal unemployment relief. The tariff raise was partly in retaliation for similar protective measures against Canadian goods in the U.S.A.; the tariff so established was the highest ever enacted in Canada.

The tariff forced the other Commonwealth countries to set up a trading system of imperial preferences. This was organized at a conference at Ottawa in 1932. The British were not easily moved in this direction, since they had been advocates of free trade for almost a century.

However, the mother country finally listed a significant number of Canadian industrial and agricultural goods which would have duty-free treatment in Britain in return for reciprocal treatment of British goods in Canada. Another feature of the conference was concrete evidence of Commonwealth internal autonomy, as individual dominions negotiated treaties with each other.

The Bennett actions had the short-term effect of some increase in Canadian production and inter-Commonwealth trade. But Canada needed extensive trade with the U.S.A. and continental Europe to maintain a healthy economy; this was not possible in the existing circumstances of international depression and a high protectionist tariff. The latter made it more difficult for European countries to market their goods in Canada, thereby earning currency to buy Canadian goods. The U.S.A. itself had a high restrictive tariff which cut down any possibility of maintaining trade, let alone expanding it. As a result, by 1932, Canadian conditions had resumed their progress to the depths of the depression.

In 1934, the Bank of Canada was established to administer credit and currency. The wartime Canadian Wheat Board was reactivated to control the sale of wheat.

There were federal subsidies to provinces in the economic doldrums. Other economic and commercial activity at the federal level included the organization of Trans-Canada Airlines (now Air Canada), the re-organization of Canadian National Railways, and the inauguration of the Canadian Broadcasting Corporation.

At the same time, Bennett's Minister of Trade and Commerce, H.H. Stevens, was advocating somewhat extreme measures of business control for a Conservative. He was anxious for price control to be established and thought that some large retail organizations were profiteering by excessive price margins, largely made possible by grossly underpaying producers.

He persuaded Bennett to set up a Royal Commission on Price Spreads. Stevens, however, was too radical for his cabinet colleagues. he left the administration in 1935 and formed the abortive Reconstruction party.

For the 1935 election, it was clear that the country demanded drastic efforts to curb the worst effects of the depression. Bennett decided to imitate Roosevelt's New Deal in the U.S.A., and proposed a program of regulation of business, minimum rates of pay and maximum hours, regulation of the export trade, reduction of farm debt and the inception of a system of unemployment insurance.

## 2. Provincial Party Politics
### a. Social Credit

The Social Credit movement began in Alberta. It was based on the theories of an Englishman, Major Douglas, who had advocated a governmental cash payment or "social dividend" to all members of the community. The money was to come from the governmental exploitation of natural resources on behalf of the people.

The organizer and leader in Alberta was a former radio preacher, William Aberhart. He began political activities in 1934, mixing Social Credit, drama, and fundamental religion, together with a hypnotic delivery.

In the 1935 provincial election in Alberta, Social Credit was brought to power. Aberhart rapidly found out that the practice of many of his theories was unconstitutional. The courts turned many of them down. Finally, he concentrated more on good conventional government and less on his theories.

## b. The Co-Operative Commonwealth Federation (CCF)

There had been a small labor party in existence, at the federal level since 1919. J.S. Woodsworth was its leader at Ottawa. Its socialist policies suddenly became more attractive after the depression had struck, finding an audience principally among the farmers, artisans, union leaders and some intellectuals.

In 1932, these groups met at Calgary and formed the Co-operative Commonwealth Federation (CCF). In 1933, a platform of Canadian socialism was embarked upon. It included nationalization of the major features of the Canadian economy, together with federal reorganization of trade and commerce.

## c. The Union Nationale

After 1920, Quebec entered a period of industrialization. Most of the necessary financing had been done outside the province. As a result, when the depression struck, there was some feeling that the French Canadian worker had been let down by foreign corporations.

The rump of the Quebec Conservative party and a group of dissident Liberals agreed on a program of social welfare and the provincialization of some foreign-owned properties. The new party called itself the Union Nationale. The leader was Maurice Duplessis, who had been a Conservative.

By 1936, the Union Nationale had taken power in the province from the Liberals, aided by the latter's corruption. In power, Duplessis overlooked the social reforms and, instead, raised the bogey of federal threats to the French Canadian identity. This resulted in a hostile attitude towards the national government for many years in Quebec.

In British Columbia, the provincial Liberal party, led by Pattullo, took the election of 1933 on a program of "Work and Wages" — another echo of Roosevelt's New Deal. The program called for financial help to depressed industries, provincial works projects, relief, and the usual minimum wages and maximum hours legislation.

Implementation of the program necessarily caused a provincial deficit. There was an appeal to the federal government for funds. For the rest of the depression, British Columbia, too, was committed to arguing with the federal government amid increasing bitterness.

# 3. Autonomy

The Statute of Westminster (1931) for all practical purposes rounded out Canadian autonomy. This British legislation gave Canada and all the dominions power to pass extra-territorial laws, laid down that no British law would henceforward have any binding power in the dominions and withdrew the Colonial Laws Validity Act (1865) which stipulated that in a conflict with any colonial law, the British law would be supreme.

There remained some vestiges of British power, but only because Canada so desired. The British Judicial Committee of the Privy Council remained the final court of appeal for Canadians — hence, the interpreter of the constitution. Amendments to the Canadian constitution still needed to be enacted by the parliament at Westminster.

One result of the Statute was that the Governor-General ceased to be the representative of the British government, and became the personal representative of the Crown.

It should be remembered that the slow advent of Canadian autonomy had received support from all parties who had held power since Confederation.

## 4. Foreign Relations

Many Canadians believed that they could remain isolated from Europe and the rest of the world. When in 1931, Japan entered Manchuria the attention of the western powers, including Canada, was on combatting the depression. There was no urgent cry to help China.

It was not until the succeeding administration, however, that the problem of the dictators began to gain the attention of the League and the Western democracies.

## 5. The Election of 1935

Bennett and the Conservatives campaigned with a program closely copied from that of Roosevelt in the U.S.A. (see above). The Liberals, however, made the point that much of the promised legislation would be unconstitutional and could be appealed through the courts. King was also opposed to the high tariff, arguing that any apparent protection was false, since it really prevented trade rather than protected it.

The Liberals put their own program of reform forward. It seemed more practicable to the electorate, who felt that Bennett's change of heart had come too late. As it turned out, the Liberals merely retained their popular vote, making few converts. However, the new splinter parties had all gained supporters at the expense of the Conservatives. The Liberals, then, were returned with an overwhelming absolute majority of more than one hundred seats.

# XIX. King's Liberals Return to Power, 1935-1945

## 1. Federal-Provincial Relations

King's attempts to relieve the depression in Canada rapidly exposed the anachronistic state of the federal-provincial system. He had begun by handing Bennett's proposed New Deal to the courts for an opinion on its constitutionality. He had then negotiated a trade treaty with the U.S.A. which loosened the restrictions on the entry of Canadian products to the U.S. market and reduced the Canadian tariff on some U.S. imports.

This scarcely alleviated the slump, but shortly afterwards the Supreme Court handed down its decision that much of Bennett's legislation would have been unconstitutional. The implication was that under the constitution as established in 1867, the federal government lacked the power to help the individual Canadian citizen to the best of its ability.

In that case, the constitution was as much to blame as the depression. King, therefore, set up a royal commission (1937) to investigate the entire area of dominion-provincial relations. It is known as the Rowell-Sirois Commission, after its two chairmen.

It was three years before the Commission made its final report. By that time, Canada was involved in World War II, and the country was well on its way out of the depression. The Commission found that the constitution had been affected by two major circumstances. First, a succession of interpretations by the Judicial Committee of the (British) Privy Council had reduced the authority of the federal government; secondly, changed circumstances had brought tremendously increased responsibilities to the provinces which could not have been foreseen by the Fathers of Confederation, particularly in the expansion of social services. In other words, the constitution no longer completely suited the twentieth century.

The net result was that the federal government had the power to raise ample funds to defeat the social distress of the depression, but it did not have the authority to decide where these funds were to be disposed in the provinces. On the other hand, the provinces had the power, but insufficient financial sources.

The Commission's recommendation was that the federal government's powers should be broadened, particularly to apply some form of uniform welfare to the country, and some measure of control over the country's economy at the provincial level.

This was to be done by giving the Ottawa government exclusive rights of direct taxation. In return for this, the dominion government would make subsidies available to the provinces to maintain minimum standards of welfare and social services. The aim was to remove sectional inequalities. Specifically and urgently, it recommended the federal government ought to move into unemployment insurance and relief.

The less wealthy provinces were naturally delighted by the Commission's recommendations; the more endowed ones were less so.

Quebec, British Columbia and Ontario were certain to lose, on balance.

However, the federal government is always capable of taking increased powers in emergency, and the country was now at war. Although Alberta, British Columbia and Ontario declined formally to go into the report at a dominion-provincial conference (1941), the national government was able to make individual arrangements with each province as regards tax sharing.

By that time, however, the money was needed for war purposes, not welfare. As far as social finance was concerned, the electorate had to be satisfied with a constitutional amendment in 1940 which empowered the federal government to set up an unemployment insurance scheme. Later federal governments used this as a precedent for such national welfare schemes as children's allowances.

## 2. Foreign Relations

In 1935, Mussolini, the Italian dictator, invaded Ethiopia. The League of Nations administered economic sanctions, which, however, excluded oil, a vital war material. It was clear that such sanctions could not seriously affect a country's war potential.

The Canadian representative at Geneva, Dr. Riddell, put forward the suggestion that oil sanctions should be imposed. Unfortunately, since the U.S.A. was not a member of the League, and since U.S. companies were delivering oil to Mussolini in U.S. ships, it was clear to King that a situation might develop whereby a Canadian warship might be forced to take hostile action against a U.S. vessel.

This eventuality, King was not prepared to accept. He repudiated Riddell, insisting that the Canadian delegate had been speaking for himself, not Canada. There was some truth in this, for most Canadians were not anxious to become involved in European problems. Another bogey which haunted King was the possibility that such an involvement might again bring about the ethnic cleavage such as had occurred over conscription in 1917, and from which the country had scarcely started to recover.

In the same way, King supported Chamberlain's so-called appeasement of Hitler in 1938. He may thus be accused of having been overcautious, but in this he was merely copying the policy of greater powers who might have been expected to have been more responsible. As it was, when the Germans invaded Poland on September 1, 1939, thus starting World War II, Canada was almost entired unprepared.

However, the country had achieved control over her own external affairs since the outbreak of World War I. Consequently, Britain declared war on Germany on September 3, 1939 but Canada waited one week, until parliament could be summoned, before formally committing herself.

## 3. Canada and World War II

It appeared to be a united country which had entered the War. If so, it was the result of two decades of cautious avoidance of any issues which might be divisive. As a result, support for the war effort was basically united.

### a. Military

It appeared, in 1939, that the Canadian participation would be mainly in the form of materials and machines. After the defeat of Poland had shown the power of the Nazi war machine, it was clear that Canadian troops would be needed, and contingents began to proceed to Britain.

During the Battle of Britain, 1940, the only organized infantry divisions in Britain were those from Canada, which had not been committed to action in the campaigns in France (which had led to Dunkirk). In 1941, two battalions were sent to Hong Kong, only to be lost in a few days at Christmas, 1941.

In August, 1942, Canadian troops landed at Dieppe in France in a costly invasion experiment. In July, 1943, a Canadian division landed in Sicily, and another joined it in Italy a few months later. On June 6, 1944, Canadian forces landed on the coast of France in the final Allied invasion of Europe (D-Day). When the European campaign ended in May, 1945, Canadian forces, for the first time, were organized as a Canadian Army.

The Royal Canadian Navy had the major share in guarding the convoys on the North Atlantic run. The Royal Canadian Air Force fought in all theaters of the War. The British Commonwealth Air Training Scheme, with most of its centers in Canada, trained thousands of Allied airmen.

Canada played an important military role in the defeat of the Axis powers. It is generally forgotten that at the end of the War, Canada was the world's fourth greatest military power, following the U.S.A., the U.S.S.R. and Britain.

### b. Conscription

Generally, French Canada supported the Canadian posture at the beginning of the war. At the same time, it was clear that it would never accept compulsory military service overseas. Its representatives at Ottawa agreed with this attitude. The French-Canadian attitude can be summarized as backing for the war effort, with all army service outside Canada to be voluntary.

Since the federal government had given assurances on conscription, the provincial Liberal party was able to capture Quebec from the Union Nationale in October, 1939, and the federal election in 1940.

Dunkirk and its aftermath caused the cry of conscription to be raised again, and legislation was passed bringing it in for service in Canada only. However, when the U.S.A. came into the War in late 1941, with its draft for overseas service, the demand for a similar contribution began again in Canada.

Finally, in April 1942, the federal government organized a plebiscite to ask the electorate to release it from the undertaking to avoid conscription for overseas. It was made clear that this did not mean that such conscription would begin at once, or even at all. The government merely wanted the power to proceed when it felt the occasion had arisen.

Predictably, about three-quarters of Quebec opposed the release; a rather higher proportion of the rest of the country accepted the new position. King postponed any immediate action, thus postponing any possible crisis.

After D-Day it was obvious that voluntary enlistments were not keeping the units up to strength. The wounded and sick volunteers in action were being returned to their units before they were completely fit. The Minister of Defence resigned from the cabinet when King still refused conscription for overseas.

In November, 1944, however, in the face of a cabinet crisis, King allowed limited conscription to go forward. As it turned out, the outcry was slight and there was no hostile division as in 1917. Actually, conscripts only reached action in small numbers. Canadian casualties overseas included only two dozen dead conscript soldiers throughout the entire war.

King's policy of caution and waiting had thus been completely vindicated. His main lieutenant from Quebec, Louis St. Laurent, supported him throughout and later took command of the Liberal party.

## 4. U.S.-Canadian Relations

As war became imminent, the U.S. and Canada relations improved. After the fall of France, while Britain was under air attack, King and Roosevelt met at Ogdensburg, New York where Roosevelt guaranteed that Canada would not fall into the hands of any European power should Britain fall. At the same time, it was decided that North America should be considered as a common defence unit. The Permanent Joint Board on Defence was set up for the study of mutual action and problems. Measures for co-operation in the event of attack were decided upon.

Later, Canada acted as the mediator in the Anglo-American agreement (1940) whereby Britain received fifty over-age destroyers in return for bases in the western Atlantic. Also in 1940, U.S. engineers began the construction of a military road through Canada to Alaska (the Alaskan Highway).

King met Roosevelt again in April, 1941. From this meeting came the Hyde Park Declaration, which called for increased purchases of war supplies by the U.S. in Canada and co-operation in defence production. World War II, therefore, brought a measure of fusion to the economies of the two countries.

### 5. Foreign Relations

Canada's foreign relations during the war were almost entirely dictated by her membership in the Commonwealth and, later, the United Nations. When the War ended in August, 1945, it was clear to most Canadians that it would no longer be possible to return to the isolation and limited League membership of the between-the-wars years. Accordingly, it was with the full support of the people that Canada became a charter member of the United Nations Organization.

During the War, Canada's autonomy had allowed her to maintain a representative in Vichy, France after the British had broken off relations (and sunk part of its fleet).

## XX. The Liberals Retain Power, 1945-1957

### 1. Federal Affairs

King called a federal election just before the end of the War in June, 1945. The Liberals lost a few seats, but remained in office with an absolute majority. Generally, Quebec supported King, as did the Maritimes. The Conservatives had 47 seats in Ontario, but only 19 in other provinces. Alberta was Social Credit, and Saskatchewan went over to the CCF, which was unsuccessful elsewhere.

In 1946, the offices of Prime Minister and External Affairs Secretary were divided. King chose Louis St. Laurent for the latter post.

In 1948, King retired, dying in 1950. He was succeeded as Prime Minister by St. Laurent, who held the office until the defeat of the Liberal party in the federal election of 1957.

In 1947, the Governor-General, Field-Marshal Lord Alexander of Tunis, (a British soldier who had commanded Canadian troops in World War II, and who was Canada's last British Governor-General), was given the complete right to all the privileges of the British Crown in Canada. In 1952, Alexander was succeeded by Vincent Massey, a Canadian.

During those early post-war years, a formal Canadian citizenship was established (1947) as being separate from British citizenship; through it Britons were not automatically Canadians, and a Canadian passport became necessary. The use of the title, dominion, gradually ceased during this period.

In 1949, it was decided to abolish the right of Canadians to appeal the decisions of the Supreme Court of Canada to the Judicial Committee of the British Privy Council. This necessarily made the Canadian court the final court of appeal for Canadians, and, as such, the body to interpret the British North America Act of 1867 and succeeding constitutional legislation. There remained, however, exceptions to the power of Canada to amend its own constitution, particularly in the fields of provincial rights in connection with language and education. These still require an act of the British parliament. Still, all the completely federal parts of the Canadian constitution are now totally under Canadian control.

Probably the major federal development in the early post-war years was the inclusion of the British colony of Newfoundland as Canada's tenth province. This occurred on March 31, 1949. The leading spirit of the pro-Confederation element on the island was J.R. (Joey) Smallwood, who remained as its premier.

Newfoundland's future had been under discussion since 1945. The main choices were either to remain as a British colony, become an independent country, join the U.S.A., or confederate with Canada. Both Canada and Great Britain were anxious that Newfoundland should join Canada, but as late as January, 1948, the convention charged with working out the island's future had requested that only two choices be placed before the island in a referendum — responsible government within the Commonwealth, or government by commission.

The British Government added the third choice of confederation with Canada on its own initiative. The people themselves were split on the issue. They realized that the finances of the island were incapable of providing the welfare services, such as unemployment insurance, family allowances, certain forms of pension for handicapped people, which were coming into service in Canada. On the other hand, there was a legacy of antipathy to Ottawa.

The first referendum gave responsible government a slight edge over confederation, with a continuance of the commission government a poor third. This choice was omitted from a second referendum, at which there was a slight popular majority for confederation.

When Newfoundland joined Canada, the federal government took over the island's public debt. Other inherited problems were the U.S. military bases, a poor educational system, an economy tied to fishing, railways and a ferry unlikely to operate without generating losses, and the possibility of the loss of the better-educated and skilled Newfoundlanders to the mainland as emigrants. On the credit side, Canada obtained a strategic island with immense mineral and forest reserves. There was also the satisfaction of rounding out the country envisaged in 1867.

In 1953, the Liberals retained their power in the federal election, winning 173 of 265 seats in the House. They had managed to keep their image as a welfare party by measures such as the Old Age Security Act of 1951, by which old age pensions were brought in. It appeared unlikely that any of the federal parties in opposition would be able to remove the Liberals (although British Columbia went over to Social Credit in 1952). Later, however, the Liberals were defeated.

In 1956, the party proposed to enact a statute which would enable the Trans-Canada pipeline (for natural gas) to be built with the aid of a federal grant; the company operating the line, however, was under the control of a U.S. company. There was nothing particularly unusual about this. Unfortunately, the government high-handedly stifled debate on the matter in the Commons by the use of "closure". By this device, debate must end at a certain deadline, this to be fixed by the government. It was a tactic rarely used until then.

The opposition parties were doubtful of the pipeline financing, but their principal objection was to the use of closure. The Conservative party had, in the same year, chosen John G. Diefenbaker, a Prairie lawyer, as its leader. He was able to present himself to the electorate, in the period leading up to 1957 federal election, as the defender of parliamentary government, at the same time inculcating into the Conservatives a measure of spirit and some hope that the tide might at last turn.

## 2. Federal-Provincial Affairs

The main federal-provincial problem was financial: the organization of the financing of the welfare schemes was introduced by the federal government during the period. The objects of the schemes themselves were within the powers of the provincial governments, who were unable or unwilling to finance them. There was also the usual fear, especially in Ontario, Quebec and British Columbia, of the loss of internal power to federal encroachment.

If the provinces were to finance their own schemes, they would require a larger share of the federal tax income. The Rowell-Sirois Commission (see above) had earlier placed its recommendations before the country, but there was little hope that they would be accepted by all the provinces. In 1947, however, Ottawa was able to negotiate a new tax-sharing agreement, to run for five years, with all the provinces except Ontario and Quebec.

Later agreements were made in 1952 and 1957, both of which Ontario joined; Quebec, however, remained adamant in opposition.

In 1957, just before the fall of the Liberals, the Supreme Court of Canada nullified the so-called Padlock Act. This was a Quebec provincial statute by which officers of the provincial government could, without normal democratic legal process, cause any premises to be closed at will. Supposedly an anti-communist measure, it had been used by the Quebec government in personal and religious vendettas, particularly by Premier Duplessis.

## 3. The Gouzenko Case

In September, 1945, Igor Gouzenko, a code clerk at the U.S.S.R. Embassy in Ottawa, sought political asylum in Canada. When he left his post he brought with him documentary proof of the operation of a Soviet spy ring in Canada. This was at a time when the U.S.S.R. was a formal ally of Canada.

It appeared that the ring had been operating since work had been started in Canada on atomic research, in 1942. It had enjoyed some success and had been able to recruit British and Canadian scientists as informants.

Gouzenko's story was investigated in secrecy and the trails led to the U.S.A. and Britain. As a result, in all these countries arrests were made and spy networks broken up. The affair was made public in June, 1964, and it was one of the opening battles in the "Cold War". There is no doubt that the case profoundly affected Canadian opinion, leading to a wider acceptance of UNO commitments and eventual membership in NATO.

## 4. The Economy

The Canadian economy boomed after World War II. There were many reasons for the boom, which affected practically every section of the economy and the community. During the War, Canadian industry had expanded but had received no damage. There was a ready-made market for consumer goods, to make up for the wartime suspension of the production of those goods. At the same time, there was a backlog of six years' orders in such sections of the economy as construction of schools, roads, and other public works.

There were, however, deeper reasons for economic growth than catching up with delayed orders. The population had grown. There was a new and continued influx of immigrants ("New Canadians"), who provided both a market and a labor force. The country, with its established stability, was attractive to foreign capital, so much so, that U.S. investments became so large as to be a problem.

Primary industry continued to be the backbone of the country's economy. Pulp and paper remained as the greatest single contributor. The newsprint section alone grew until it produced almost 50 per cent of the world's total.

The discovery of high-grade iron ore deposits on the Shield (the first major find had been at Steep Rock in 1938) coincided with the dwindling of U.S. resources. By the early 1950's, the project at Knob Lake in Quebec was under way. New communications and harbors were built to handle the product. The market expanded to include Japan (supplied from British Columbia).

Other, more exotic minerals founded flourishing industries. Potash — one of the largest deposits in the world — started being mined in Saskatchewan. There was a uranium boom based on research into atomic power and atomic armament. This industry faded, as the stockpiles grew too big in the late 1959's. Steel production, nickel mining and aluminum processing also expanded rapidly.

The greatest success story is probably that of the oil and natural gas industry. This virtually began on February 13, 1947, when Imperial Oil's Leduc No. 1 well gushed oil. A frenzy of geological exploration began, which revealed oilfields under much of Western Canada, particularly Alberta.

By the end of the Liberal administration, Canada had not only become self-sufficient in oil (before the war the country had imported almost 100 per cent of its needs), but was about to begin exporting to the former suppliers.

Natural gas was found with the oil and this grew into a powerful industry in its own right, with secondary industries such as sulphur extraction. A pipeline complex was undertaken. By 1953, oil was being pumped 2,000 miles from Edmonton to Sarnia, Ontario, and into the U.S.A. Gas also was being carried into Eastern Canada, and the U.S. Northwest and Midwest.

Agriculture flourished; Europe had to be fed. This, too, was an industry which experienced something of a recession after the boom. The seller's market lasted until 1952, after which there was something of a lagging market until after the fall of the Liberal administration.

In the field of transportation and communications, the greatest development was the construction of the St. Lawrence Seaway. Connected with the transportation project was a hydro-electrical complex. The aim was to connect the Great Lakes with oceanic shipping.

As early as 1932, the U.S.A. and Canada had agreed that such a project should be entered upon in the future. Vested transport interests in the U.S.A. had been able to block any active measures, however. By 1950, Canada felt capable of proceeding independently, and so advised the U.S.A. This forced a decision upon the larger country. In 1954, Congress committed the U.S.A. to the project.

The Seaway was actually opened after the Liberals left power (in 1959). It has completely altered the form of the Lakes' traffic.

## 5. Culture

The Massey Report (1951) was the result of a Royal Commission on National Development in the Arts, Letters and Sciences, set up in 1949. The Commission found that the federal government ought to make itself more responsible for the development of a national culture.

The Report coincided with an awakened interest in a national culture and identity and focussed private and public interest on it. Private and semi-private enterprises such as the Stratford Shakespearean Festival (1953) began. The work of the National Film Board and the Canadian Broadcasting Corporation was confirmed and expanded.

The Report recommended the inauguration of the Canada Council, to encourage and patronize the arts and sciences. This was done in 1957. An earlier start had been made in 1952 with significant federal grants to universities (refused by the Quebec universities after the first year).

## 6. Foreign Affairs

Canada was a charter member of the United Nations Organization in 1945. The Cold War emphasized the Canadian commitment to that body, and public opinion tended to accept increased participation and commitment to its work, so much so that Canada was often one of the initiators of UN activity and intervention.

The Canadian attitude was that the smaller powers have their part to play, not always as supporters of particular blocs or individual countries. The first post-war commitment (the War against Japan was still going on when the UNO was formed), was a charter membership in the North Atlantic Treaty Organization (NATO). This alliance arose partly out of a suggestion by the Canadian Minister for External Affairs, Louis St. Laurent.

The aim of the organization is mutual defence against Soviet aggression. Remarkably, however, the two North American members, Canada and the U.S.A., committed themselves to a defence line in Europe. Since that time, both Canadian and U.S. units have been components in a co-ordinated defence system based in Western Europe and its waters.

The Treaty also contains provisions for economic and cultural cooperation between its members, again largely at Canadian insistence. The Canadian ideal of an Atlantic community, however, has been more apparent than real.

The Canadian readiness to help solve international problems was increasingly shown. When the Korean War broke out in July, 1950, Canada at once supported UNO action, then committed troops to a total of a brigade. Canada suffered almost 2,000 casualties, including 400 dead.

At this time, also, Canada strongly backed the planning and implementation of the Colombo Plan. This was a plan by which nonwhite emerging nations of the Commonwealth in Africa and Asia were to receive economic assistance from the older Commonwealth countries. The aim was to encourage these newer countries to contain the spread of communism by their own efforts and economic recovery.

Among other forms of assistance has been that of a nuclear generating station to India, ships, locomotives, schools and teachers, and help in constructing dams. Canada has made a total contribution of some half-billion dollars to the Colombo Plan.

In 1954, Canada agreed to assist in the execution of the cease-fire agreement in French Indo-China (now Vietnam), together with Poland and India. This participation demonstrated the developing Canadian philosophy of commitment in areas remote from Canada, in the interests of international peace.

Canada has continued to be actively interested in the work of the Disarmament Commission of the United Nations and its subcommittee. Another UNO venture from which Canada emerged with credit during this period was its support, in 1955, of the admission of sixteen out of eighteen applicants for membership of that body. Paul Martin was the leader of the Canadian delegation at the time.

Canada was a non-permanent member of the Security Council of the United Nations twice during this period — in 1947 and 1957. During the formative years of the Organization, many Canadians served in positions of authority. Lester B. Pearson was active in the establishment of peace-keeping machinery, while the first director of WHO was a Canadian, Brock Chisholm, as was the first Director-General of the UN Technical Assistance Administration, Hugh Keenleyside. General Burns was more or less continuously committed to work with the UNO.

In 1956, the invasion of Suez by Britain and France caused Canada to oppose British actions openly at the UNO meetings. Pearson then introduced his resolution which resulted in the dispatch of a force to keep the peace in the area, after the withdrawal of the invading troops. This force, the United Nations Expeditionary Force (UNEF), remained in the area until 1967 and set a precedent for later interventions by UNO. Pearson received the Nobel Peace Prize in 1957 for his work in the UNO.

U.S.-Canada relations continued to involve a high degree of co-operation (see St. Lawrence Seaway, above). It became apparent that the northern defence zone of the U.S.A. lay over Canada. As a result, the Permanent Joint Board on Defence was reactivated. Further measures of mutual defence, particularly against the attacks by manned bombers over the North Pole, followed. These included the construction of three roughly parallel chains of radar defences across Canada — the Pine Tree Line, the Distant Early Warning (DEW) Line and, later, the Mid-Canada, or McGill Line. These lines have gradually been abandoned as the threat of the missile has superseded that of the bomber.

In 1957, a formal arrangement was inaugurated known as

NORAD (North American Air Defence Agreement). Through this, certain air defence units of both the U.S. and Canadian services are under the command of a joint structure located at Colorado Springs. It is the convention that the deputy commander of the system is a Canadian officer; as a result, it is often the case that the defence of the entire North American continent is under the responsibility of a Canadian in uniform.

An increasingly significant feature of U.S.-Canada relations, however, was the rapid increase of U.S. investments in Canadian development and industry. There was the natural fear that whoever controlled the economy controlled the country. There was also the prospect of some form of economic union which might well lead to political union.

By 1956, U.S. residents controlled over one-half of Canadian industry, by value of investment, and the rate of new investment in Canada was even higher, approaching three-quarters. Some industries, especially the newer types such as oil and gas, were almost completely dominated by U.S. capital.

In 1957, the Gordon Royal Commission on the Canadian Economy recommended that Canadians should be given an opportunity to buy the common stock of U.S. subsidiaries operating in Canada. This has been brought into effect by many of the companies concerned. The Commission also wished to see native Canadians in more of the executive positions in those companies.

As a result of the report, some statutes appeared on the books protecting ownership of Canadian banks from falling into the hands of U.S. residents and putting restrictions on advertising in U.S. magazines.

## 7. The Provinces

Alberta became extremely prosperous in the post-war economic boom. The climate and trade cycle effect on wheat was completely smoothed out by provincial control of the oilfields. By this, the province took a royalty on each barrel of crude oil; the funds were first used to reduce the provincial debt and then to subsidize extensive welfare schemes.

In Quebec, Duplessis and the Union Nationale had been returned to power in 1944, and remained until after the sudden death of Duplessis in 1959. He had retained his opposition to co-operation with the federal government in such matters as education and the Canadianization of the constitution as regards education and language. Generally, his administration was marked by ultra-conservatism and corruption.

The CCF maintained its control of Saskatchewan, gained in 1944, with T.C. Douglas as premier. After 1952, both Alberta and British

Columbia had Social Credit administrations.

## 8. The Election of 1957

The Liberals were defeated in the general election on June 10, 1957. They gained 104 seats whereas the Conservatives won 109. Social Credit had 19 and the CCF 25. As a result, Louis St. Laurent resigned and the Conservative leader, John Diefenbaker, was able to form a government.

There were many reasons for the downfall of the Liberals. The immediate cause was the uproar over the pipeline debate and closure (see above). There were, however, deeper causes. There was the groundswell of opinion that "it was time for a change." The grain market had become flabby and the western farmers had lost confidence in the Liberals. Other branches of the economy were upset at the tight money policy of the Bank of Canada, controlled by the government. The recent Gordon Report had suggested that Maritimers might well solve their problems by moving into other provinces and this had caused some dissatisfaction in that area.

There was also the undercurrent of anti-Americanism, exploited by Diefenbaker, aroused by the Liberals' apparent tenderness towards U.S. interests generally, and particularly in the episode of the pipeline. St. Laurent resigned from leadership of the Liberal party on its defeat, and was succeeded by Lester Pearson.

# XXI. Diefenbaker's Conservatives in Power, 1957-1963

## 1. The Election of 1958

Diefenbaker decided to push a series of reform and welfare measures through the Commons, with his slim majority. He was able to increase old-age pensions and organize subsidies for Maritime power projects, and for grain harvested and stored on the farms.

As well as these practical measures, he was able to put before the country practical evidence of his party's looking to the future. In October, 1957, he set up a royal commission under Henry Borden to enquire into the best future use of Canada's resources, especially coal, oil, gas, water and uranium.

Armed with these successes, he asked for a dissolution and went to the country. In the resulting election the Conservatives won a complete and crushing victory. They gained 209 seats, including 50 in Quebec. The Liberals dwindled to 48 seats, and the minority parties ceased to be effective units, only the CCF gaining 8 seats. To date, it is the greatest landslide victory in Canadian federal politics.

## 2. The Economy
A recession followed the second election, and its effects were felt more or less throughout the whole administration. One casualty was the aircraft industry; in 1959, work was abandoned on Canada's own fighter aircraft, the Avro Arrow.

Unemployment grew steadily; the new government seemed unable to come to grips with the minor slump. This was mainly because the causes lay outside the country. There was a diminution of U.S. investment, because there was something of a recession there. The European industrial market had slumped, partially because Canada could not meet the price competition, and partly because European recovery was almost complete.

The fall in exports, however, caused an increasing balance of payments problem which hounded the economy. Finally, in 1962, the Canadian dollar was devalued in reference to the U.S. dollar and pegged at about $92 1/2$ U.S. cents. This enabled many industries, notably pulp and paper, to compete effectively in the U.S. Market.

The agricultural section of the economy, however, flourished. This was partly because of the Conservative subsidies, but two bad harvests in 1959-60 caused the moving of the surpluses of the late 1950's. At the same time, new overseas markets opened up, particularly in the U.S.S.R. and China.

Trade problems caused the organization (1960) of the National Productivity Council, which had the two aims of finding methods of increasing productivity and trade, and encouraging the co-operation of labor and management.

The welfare state was taken over by the Conservatives, and their legislation included increases in various pensions, such as those paid to veterans, the disabled and the old. To pay for these and other developments, new federal-provincial tax agreements were negotiated. One significant welfare scheme at the provincial level was the entry of the Ontario government into pre-paid hospital care.

## 3. Federal Politics
In 1960, the Indians received the federal franchise. More publicized, but actually less weighty, was the 1960 Canadian Bill of Rights. Diefenbaker made himself personally responsible for the enactment of this statute, which appeared to copy the British and U.S. bills of rights in granting such ancient inalienable liberties as freedom of speech, habeas corpus, and similar protections. In actual fact, it was merely a recitation of the liberties which Canadians had already gained over the years.

Other federal legislation included the organization of the Board of Broadcast Governors, to oversee both radio and television, statutes to assist Canadian magazines, and the organization of plans to open up the north by transportation schemes. The South Saskatchewan River irrigation and power complex was begun.

In 1962, the Trans-Canada Highway was finally opened, so that an all-weather route existed across Canada from Halifax to Vancouver entirely on Canadian soil. In the same year, the Canadian satellite Alouette was launched by a U.S. rocket from a U.S. base in California.

## 4. Foreign Affairs

Within the Commonwealth, two main issues presented themselves to the administration during its period in office. When it appeared likely that Britain might enter the European Common Market, Diefenbaker demanded a Commonwealth conference before a definite British commitment was made. As it turned out, France opposed British participation, thus barring Britain's entry.

The other issue was the problem presented by the opposition of the non-white members of the Commonwealth to the apartheid policies of the South African government. Diefenbaker took the position of complete opposition to this policy; South Africa accordingly left the Commonwealth in 1960.

Despite acceptance of the NORAD agreement with the U.S.A. — it was actually signed by the Conservative government — Diefenbaker took the apparently illogical step of refusing to accept nuclear warheads for anti-aircraft rockets based in Canada as part of the defence system. At the same time, nuclear weapons were refused for Canada's forces in NATO.

Canada, however, continued to support the work of UNO. In 1960, a force of Canadian troops and airmen was sent to the Congo (formerly the Belgian Congo and known today as Zäire), to help solve the chaos which followed the arrival of self-government there and the resulting UNO intervention.

At the UN meetings and at the Geneva Disarmament Conference, Canada continued to press for organized disarmament. Efforts were aimed particularly at a nuclear testing ban and some formula for arms' reduction. The Minister of External Affairs, Howard Green, often attended meetings and led the Canadian delegation.

## 5. The Fall of the Conservatives, 1962-63

There was a gradual loss of support for the Conservatives throughout their second administration. They maintained power after the general election of 1962 only with difficulty, and were defeated in 1963. The 1962 election was the start of a six-year period of minority government.

The causes for the change were complex. Within the Conservative party there was a serious split. It is not too much to say that Diefenbaker's administration disintegrated on him. One decisive factor was the issue of nuclear arms for defence; his indecision on this matter alienated his own defence minister, who resigned.

Diefenbaker was entirely unable to recruit a French-Canadian leader of sufficient stature to hold Quebec for the party when the tide began to run against it. At the same time, there was a resurgence in the provincial Liberal party, which offered a new program to take the place of the Union Nationale, shattered by the death of Duplessis and, shortly afterwards, his successor.

In 1960, in the Quebec provincial election, the Liberals, led by Lesage, defeated the Union Nationale. Soon afterwards, there was a growth of interest in Social Credit in the province, and by the 1962 election there was a significant strength to this group on the federal scene, led by Réal Caouette. The western branch of the federal party itself had picked a new leader in 1961, Robert Thompson from Alberta.

A new force on the federal political scene had also been created by the formation of a left-wing party on the ruins of the old CCF party. The trade unions supported a platform somewhat less socialist than that of the CCF. The result was the New Democratic Party (NDP), led by the former Saskatchewan Premier, T.C. Douglas. The points of its program were wider social welfare and economic planning.

Another factor in the waning popularity of Diefenbaker's party was that, probably through no fault of its own, it was unable to turn into fact the promise of a new Canadian boom. The administration was met with a recession and a higher rate of unemployment than a generation, which had not known the depression, was prepared to accept.

In the election of 1962, the wave which had swept the Conservatives into power receded. They only retained 116 seats. The Liberals staged a comeback, picking up 99 seats. Minority parties became influential with the NDP's 19 seats and Social Credit's 30, mostly in Quebec.

As a result, Diefenbaker was unable to pass legislation in the Commons which one or the other of the minority parties opposed. In 1963 he was unable to survive non-confidence motions (particularly since three of his own cabinet members had resigned) and was forced to seek dissolution. There had also been another economic crisis, during which the Canadian dollar had been devalued.

In the 1963 election the Liberals were unable to obtain an absolute majority, but won 129 seats. The Conservatives were reduced to 95, Social Credit to 24, and the NDP to 17. As a result, Canada was saddled with another minority government and Lester Pearson became Prime Minister.

# XXII. Pearson's Liberals Rule as a Minority, 1963-1968

When Pearson became Prime Minister, he was faced with the problems of being the leader of a minority government, an economic recession, a growing separatist sentiment in Quebec, some feeling of conflict between the industrial and agricultural interests, and the aftermath of indecision in foreign and defence policies.

## 1. The Economy

Pearson's financial expert, Walter Gordon, introduced a nationalist budget in 1963, but was unable to force it through the Commons in its original form; it was eventually heavily amended and the sting was taken out of it.

Despite the election promises of the Liberals to quicken the rate of economic recovery, partly by economic planning at the federal and regional level, and to reduce unemployment, the party was less than completely successful. There were, however, some useful statutes to show for two year's work in 1965, when Pearson went to the country in the hope of obtaining an absolute majority.

Among these achievements was an agreement with the U.S.A. which bordered on reciprocity. This last statute removed the duties on automobile parts coming into the country, on condition that the automobile industry in Canada was not harmed.

Other economic developments within the same period were the first movement of ore out of Pine Point, N.W.T., to smelters in British Columbia, over the newly-completed stretch of the Great Slave Lake Railway, and the discovery of a huge iron ore deposit, possibly the world's greatest, on Baffin Island.

## 2. Federal-Provincial and Provincial Affairs

The Social Credit party rapidly split into two groups — the Quebec Creditistes, led by Réal Caouette, and a pathetic remnant led by Thompson. Quebec itself underwent a "quiet revolution" under the provincial Liberals, led by Lesage. Welfare schemes, especially in pensions and medical insurance, were begun, organized efforts were made to attract industry, an international exhibition (Expo '67) was organized for Montreal, Quebec power companies were provincialized, reform in education was begun and there was some financial help for culture.

Despite this program, a revived Union Nationale, led by Daniel Johnson, was able to obtain power in the provincial elections of 1966. There is no doubt that some of its success was due to an increasing nationalism within the province. During the early part of the Pearson administration the separatist movement became militant, and lives were lost in several bombing incidents in Quebec. Still, Union Nationale won on its strength in rural Quebec.

The federal government attempted to seek out the roots of the problem by appointing a Royal Commission on Biculturalism and Bilingualism. This Commission duly made its report in 1965; it was clear that radical measures were required, including some possible alteration of the constitution to account for Quebec's special position.

In Nova Scotia, the last segregated black school was closed in 1963. Later that year, a federal-provincial conference organized increases in various pensions and allowances, with the provinces taking revenue concessions.

In 1964, Quebec set up its first Ministry of Education; in the same year, Ontario organized its first Department of University Affairs. A federal act at the same time provided for interest-free loans for university students. Later that year British Columbia lent Quebec $100 million, the first time that one province had lent money to another.

In 1966, the federal government passed the Medical Care Act, providing federal funds to help the provinces establish medicare schemes for all the citizens. It was left to the provinces to decide on how these schemes would be run.

## 3. The Flag and the Armed Services

In June, 1964, the federal parliament began the lengthy debates on a Canadian flag. The arguments dragged on, session after session, whilst the business of the country was carried out by the undemocratic method of order-in-council.

Finally, in December of the same year, the entire episode was brought to a close by the use of closure. The Commons voted to give Canada a flag showing a red maple leaf on a solid white background flanked by vertical red bars.

During the same year, a highly controversial program of integrating the armed forces was set in motion by the Defence Minister, Paul Hellyer. The process proceeded more or less uneventfully until 1966. It was a clear case of Canada being an international innovator. There was also the underlying demonstration that in Canada the civilian administration was in complete control of the military.

In summer, 1966, however, the process ran into heavy controversy, when it became apparent that a group of senior officers, largely in the Navy (a service known for its regard for tradition) were more in favor of integration as a principle rather than a process involving the Navy.

Some senior officers quietly took early pensions, while others were awarded civilian status and accepted it not so quietly. Within the middle and lower ranks, however, it appeared that progress would be acceptable and the process seemed likely to continue. The aim was to cut down duplication of services so that a higher proportion of the money allowed to the services might be used for the acquisition of new weapons and equipment.

## 4. Foreign Affairs

Until the advent of large-scale American involvement in Vietnam, U.S.-Canadian affairs went more smoothly under the Pearson administration. There were, however, occasional differences when the Canadian leader publicly disagreed with some U.S. foreign policies.

Canadian anti-aircraft missiles in Canada, and Canadian aircraft in NATO, received atomic warheads from U.S. sources; these could not however, be used without Canadian co-operation.

In 1964, Canada and the U.S. finally signed the long-negotiated Columbia River Development Treaty, by which the power and water resources of the Columbia basin were allocated and organized. British Columbia appeared to be the area most likely to benefit immediately, so much so that the province was able to lend Quebec money later in the year.

In December, 1963, Canada became linked to New Zealand, Australia and Britain by means of the Trans-Pacific cable. Within the Commonwealth, Canada supported the emergence of independent Asian and African nations. In 1965, a Canadian was chosen to become the first Secretary-General of the Commonwealth Secretariat.

In 1963, Canada sent a battalion to Cyprus as part of a UN force to maintain the truce between the Turks and Greeks on that island; this force was maintained for a number of years. In the Congo, the Canadian signal formation rose to almost 400 before the UN force was disbanded in June 1964. In 1965, a Canadian general led a UN observer group to administer the truce between Pakistan and India after the renewal of fighting in Kashmir.

Internationally, Canada extended its territorial waters to twelve miles off the coast, from three, in 1964; this necessarily limited the approach of foreign fishing fleets to twelve miles.

# XXIII. Trudeau in Power, 1968-1979

## 1. The Changing of the Guard
### a. Climate for Change

Major scandals, involving first the Liberals and then the Conservatives, had erupted in 1966 around the unrelated cases of a civil servant, George Victor Spencer, and a former Ottawa hostess, Gerda Munsinger. The charges and counter-charges hurled across the floor of the House of Commons had disillusioned Canadians with both major political parties, according to public opinion surveys taken at the time.

The Liberals called a convention to get grassroots opinion from within the party to help revitalize its image and its political ideas. Analysts did not feel that much emerged from this. The Conservatives, however, took more drastic action. In 1967, they replaced John Diefenbaker as leader of the party with Robert Stanfield, a former Premier of Nova Scotia.

In 1967, the country celebrated its 100 birthday, and change was in the air. The enormous success of Expo '67, which welcomed 50 million visitors, gave Canadians greater confidence in themselves and their country. But when President Charles De Gaulle of France came to visit Expo '67, he gave a speech in Montreal in which he used the separatist slogan, "Vive le Québec Libre." English Canadians, feeling this encouraged separatism, were outraged. French Canadians, according to surveys taken at the time did not feel that De Gaulle had necessarily endorsed separatism.

On September 18, 1967, René Levesque, a member of the provincial Liberal party, suggested that independence followed by economic union with the rest of Canada, was the only course left to Quebec. When he presented this view at a convention of the provincial Liberals, his proposal was rejected, and he and his supporters driven out of the party. Shortly after, he founded the Mouvement Souverainéte-Association, to build a new political movement in Quebec supporting independence. In 1968, his group united with the other major separatist parties to form the Parti Québecois.

Partly in response to such sentiments, the Pearson government in late 1967 invited the premiers of the provinces to Ottawa to discuss a revision of the Canadian constitution, to readjust Canadian federalism to the needs of the late twentieth century.

Social attitudes were also changing, and in 1967 the Minister of Justice, Pierre Trudeau, introduced a bill to broaden the grounds for divorce.

And finally, in June 1967, the UN peacekeeping force, including Canada's contingent, was ordered out of the Sinai Desert by Egyptian President Nasser. Soon after, war broke out between the Arabs and Israel.

Canadians believed that Canada had played a major role in peacekeeping because it was viewed as a neutral "honest broker." They found to their shock from statements made by Nasser, that Arab countries did not necessarily see Canada in that light. And the failure of the UN force to keep the peace called the concept of peacekeeping into question.

New directions in government policy were needed in many areas, Canadians believed, and new leadership must be sought.

### b. Trudeau

In 1968, many Canadians seemed to be taken by "Trudeaumania," a phrase invented by the press to describe the feeling that Pierre Elliot Trudeau elicited from the public while presenting the kind of new leadership they wanted.

Trudeau was a bachelor known for his somewhat unorthodox opinions and clothes. But he was also a French Canadian who supported federalism, and hence gained the support of many English Canadians, especially when he combatted Premier Johnson of Quebec on this issue during the federal-provincial conference of 1968. His long connection with Quebec politics, and especially the politics of the "Quiet Revolution," gave him French-Canadian support. His willingness to bring about change, shown in his divorce law, suggested that he was a man with new solutions to old problems.

Soon after he was selected to replace Lester Pearson as leader of the Liberal Party, Trudeau called an election. On June 15, 1968, Canadians gave Trudeau what they had denied Pearson: a majority government.

## 2. The Early Years, 1968-1970

### a. Social Policy

Although medicare came into effect in 1968, it was actually a product of Pearson's years in power. Passed in 1966, it was a scheme that required provincial approval and organization of services, and it was gradually applied to all Canadians. Saskatchewan, which had had its own scheme since 1962, and B.C. joined at once, followed by Newfoundland, Nova Scotia, Manitoba, Alberta, and Ontario in 1969, Quebec and P.E.I. in 1970, New Brunswick and the Northwest Territories in 1971, and the Yukon in 1972. The extent of benefits, and method of fee payments, varied from province to province. The setting of approved government fees for specified kinds of medical service was, and continues to be, a contentious issue with the medical profession.

The Omnibus Bill, introduced in 1969 to revise various aspects of the Criminal Code, seemed to have the Trudeau stamp, in that it altered the law to reflect more current social standards. Nonetheless, controversy surrounded some of its provisions for several years. Abortion was legalized in cases where the mental or physical health of the mother was involved. Gun control laws were revised, and breathalyzer tests were made legal. Parole and prison regulations were changed, and the Combines Investigation Act was altered somewhat. Homosexual acts between consenting adults were removed from the list of criminal offenses. The Omnibus Bill was adopted after five months of extended debate in the House of Commons.

In the same year, however, one of the landmark bills of the Trudeau administration was brought forward. The Official Languages Act made English and French co-equal languages in the federal civil service, Crown agencies and federal courts in bilingual districts. Bilingual districts were to be established where one of the two language groups had 10 per cent or more of the population, but these were to be established by an appointed council after careful study. A federal languages commissioner was established to investigate infractions of the law, and was to report directly to Parliament regarding the enforcement of the legislation. But the Minister of Justice declared that compulsory bilingualism was not to be established. The only purpose of the law, he stressed, was to give both language groups equal access to federal government institutions and services. Trudeau made the legislation a major part of his policy, and declared in July, 1969, that the very survival of Canada depended on the success of bilingualism.

## b. Foreign Affairs and Defence

Before Trudeau had come to power, the Department of External Affairs had started to re-examine the foreign affairs policies of Canada to see if they reflected recent changes in world affairs. Trudeau continued this review, and put his stamp on it, by making it the subject of public debate. Canada's traditional alliances, in both NATO and NORAD, were examined, and its relations with the Commonwealth, and its peacekeeping activities were subjected to searching inquiry. Canada's relations with third world countries were also examined afresh, to see if new directions ought to be taken in this area. A series of booklets was distributed to the public, as part of this debate.

The result of these examinations was a distinct shift in emphasis. The Trudeau ministry announced that, while Canada would remain in NATO, it would cut back on the troops deployed in Europe. Now that Europe's economy was flourishing, the government suggested, it was better able to look after its own defence, and had less need of Canada. Trudeau announced that the first Canadian priority, in its defence policy, would be to maintain the security, and the sovereignty, of Canadian territory. At the same time, it would explore its relationships with China, and take, perhaps, a somewhat different attitude to that power than prevailed in the United States at the time.

The Nigerian civil war, and the expulsion of Asians from Uganda, had created some disillusion in Canada about the Commonwealth. At the same time, to counter a move by Quebec to involve itself in foreign affairs, the Trudeau ministry shifted some of its attention, and aid money, to French-speaking areas of Africa.

The result of this review was not so much to drop traditional Canadian commitments, but to shift emphasis, and take a somewhat different direction than other members of the western alliance.

It seemed, however, that the government did not want to spend as much as past administrations on military hardware, and its armed forces. Certain regiments were disbanded, and the forces remaining were told that their first priority was not defence against foreign powers, but "aid to the civil power." Bases were closed, the militia was reduced, bilingualism introduced in the forces, and expensive naval vessels, notably the aircraft carrier Bonaventure, sold or scrapped.

In 1969, while this was going on, the American supertanker Manhattan was passing through the Northwest Passage to test the possibility of bringing Alaskan oil out through the Arctic Ocean. The U.S. government made it clear that it did not recognize Canadian sovereignty over the Arctic Islands, and especially in the ocean passages between them. The Canadian government passed pollution laws, demanding that vessels using these waters meet certain pollution standards before they could pass. Somewhat later, Canadian troops were sent to do manoeuvres in the high Arctic, and the government announced its intention to send patrol planes to establish its sovereignty there. But, said government critics, how could such actions be effective if the Trudeau ministry also insisted on drastic cutbacks in its armed forces? Where were the men and planes to come from?

## c. 1970

The Union Nationale government of Quebec never recovered from the death of Daniel Johnson in the late 1960's. It seemed unable to cope with economic problems in Quebec. Early in 1970, Jean-Jacques Bertrand announced a snap election which seemed to take the other parties, at first, by surprise. Separatist and nationalist parties wooed Quebec voters, but the Liberals under Robert Bourassa insisted that economic and social problems were more vital than grand gestures of Quebec nationalism. Quebec voters had become increasingly disenchanted with the Union Nationale, the party founded by Duplessis, and felt that Bourassa, an economist, could deal with pressing economic and social problems more effectively. The Liberals gained 72 seats, and the UN dropped to 17. More than that, only 19.6 per cent of Quebecers voted UN, which was virtually wiped out as a serious political party in Quebec.

The English language press outside Quebec, convinced that the province had voted for federalism and against Quebec nationalism, hailed the event as a new change for Canada.

However, 1970 was to be remembered for a different series of events.

On October 5, 1970, at 8:30 a.m., James Cross, Senior British Trade Commissioner in Montreal, was kidnapped by a cell of the Front de Liberation du Quebec, a radical separatist organization. Unless the manifesto of the FLQ was read over the radio and TV, said the FLQ,

Cross would be executed. In addition, it demanded the release of a number of imprisoned radicals as the price of Cross's release. Trudeau and Bourassa consulted immediately, and the FLQ manifesto was read to the public. But the Quebec Minister of Justice, in a TV address, rejected the demand that prisoners be released. A few minutes later, Pierre Laporte, Minister of Labour in the Bourassa government, was taken from his home by another FLQ cell. Unless the prisoners were let go, said the cell, Laporte would be killed.

Negotiations between Ottawa and Quebec continued, and between the Quebec government and the kidnappers. Federal troops were sent to protect key government installations and persons. Student demonstrations in support of the FLQ, and the urgings of prominent public figures in Quebec that negotiations with the FLQ proceed, followed this. Two days later, the War Measures Act, was declared to be in effect. This was a measure first passed during the emergency of World War I.

Membership in the FLQ was declared illegal, and 260 suspected members of the FLQ were picked up by police. Two days later the body of Pierre Laporte was found in the trunk of a car at St. Hubert Airport near Montreal.

In November, somewhat less sweeping laws were passed by Parliament to replace the War Measures Act and in December, Cross was located and freed. Towards the end of the month, three men were arrested and accused of the murder of Laporte.

Immediately after the events, opinion polls in all parts of Canada indicated massive support for Trudeau's actions. But, as historical analysis of the events of October, November and December, 1970, continues, it is clear that Trudeau's actions in 1970 may well be the most contentious issue to emerge from his administration.

## 3. Majority to Minority to Majority, 1971-1974
### a. Constitutional Change

Since early in 1968, the federal government, and the provinces, had met in a series of conferences to revise the British North America Act. Discussions were frank, and extended. In 1971, it seemed that a crucial stage had been reached.

Despite the long discussions, no agreement could be reached on major shifts in government powers. While neither the federal government, nor the provinces, were happy with the way the powers of government were divided by the BNA Act, they could not reach a consensus on how these should be changed.

Certain agreements, however, had been reached. A bill of rights had been drafted, a statement of language rights had been drawn up, and it was agreed that yearly meetings between the premiers and the prime minister of Canada should be held to discuss important areas of conflict or disagreement. And a formula had been hammered out to amend the BNA Act within Canada, without having to go to the British House of Commons to get legislation passed. Provinces, also, were to be consulted in areas where both levels of government shared power. This agreement became known as the Victoria Charter.

Quebec and Ontario wanted more power to be shifted to the provinces, but nothing could be agreed on. The federal government argued that, if the Victoria Charter were accepted by all parties, the more important changes could be discussed later.

Premier Bourassa of Quebec felt that the crisis in Quebec resulted from the continuing rise in unemployment and persistent poverty in many areas of the province. Only if the provinces gained major control over social policy, he felt, could Quebec make the changes that would defuse the crisis. But, he argued, if he agreed to the Charter, the rest of Canada would feel that enough had been done. The Charter, he pointed out, did nothing about social policy. Under pressure from all sectors of Quebec opinion, he rejected the Charter.

## b. Foreign Trade, Investment, and Policy

Economic matters became increasingly troublesome for Canada. The Canada Development Corporation was created to help Canadians gain some greater control over resource exploitation, by creating a Canadian controlled company to invest in this area. In 1971, the American government imposed a surcharge on all imports. Since two-thirds of Canada's trade was with the U.S., this hit the country hard. The Canadian government negotiated with the Americans, and for a while, it seemed that the Americans wanted substantial changes in Canadian economic policy that would be more favorable to American investment.

While this danger eased, concern over foreign investment did not, and a Foreign Investment Review Act was created in 1973 to screen new or expanding investment by foreign-owned corporations. A government board was set up to make sure such investment would really be in the best interests of Canadians. Increasingly, Canadians, at least in central Canada, were concerned that foreign investment had negative, as well as positive results.

When Canada recognized China in 1971, the government hoped that this would help to develop trade in a vast new market, and thus lessen Canadian dependence on its traditional customers. In addition, this move would, the government felt, help to ease world tensions. It may have had some role in the improved relations between China and the United States, that developed soon after.

## c. The Economy and Trudeau's Troubles

Until the 1970's, a rise in unemployment had usually been

reflected by a drop in prices. A drop in unemployment, on the other hand, had eventually been signalled by a rise in prices.

But in 1970, economists and governments all over the world were baffled as both unemployment, *and* prices, rose. The Trudeau government tried traditional economic remedies in 1971, including tax cuts, job creating programs, such as the Local Initiative Programs, and increased expenditures on government projects. They failed. Inflation, and unemployment, continued to rise.

At the same time, Canadians' estimation of the Prime Minister dropped. He seemed arrogant, unconcerned, and a little too much of a playboy. But mainly, he had failed to check inflation and unemployment. The result, in the election of 1972, was a drop in Liberal seats to 109, just two more than the Conservatives, and 23 short of a working majority.

In the following two years, Trudeau's government took a much softer line with the provinces, and seemed to be more cooperative in the constant meetings with provinces over a great range of issues. Moreover, Trudeau himself, at least in the public mind, seemed to be more chastened, less "abrasive." When the 1974 election came, brought about by the defeat of the Liberal budget, he threw himself into the election campaign with great zest.

His opponent, Robert Stanfield, appeared trapped by the same dilemma that had brought Trudeau down. The economy was still in trouble, and Stanfield urged a policy of wage and price controls. Some voters, at least, were not prepared for such a solution. Stanfield argued, with much force, that Trudeau had done nothing to solve the economic problems, and that different solutions should be tried. Nonetheless, the Liberals returned with a majority of 141 seats to the Tories' 95.

## d. Decentralization and Western Power

The Liberals had failed to win much support in western Canada in 1972, and this was true even in 1974. In western Canada, the Conservatives still held the edge in seats. For many years, western provinces had pointed out that, in order to support industries in eastern Canada, they paid higher prices for manufactured goods. Political and economic power, they said was centered east of Lake Superior.

The sudden and rapid rise of world oil prices after 1973 helped to dramatize that this situation was changing, at least for the oil-rich western provinces. As oil prices shot up, eastern Canada, especially Ontario, demanded that Canadian oil be kept below world prices. The western provinces, led by Saskatchewan, and Premier Lougheed of Alberta, insisted that the shoe was now on the other foot. Let eastern Canada, they suggested, pay higher prices for Prairie oil, just as the Prairies had always paid higher prices for eastern manufactured goods.

A long round of federal-provincial meetings kept Canadian oil prices below world figures, but they did rise dramatically, nonetheless. So did the royalties flowing into the treasuries of the western provinces. Coupled with the growth of secondary industries in Alberta, as well as new financial institutions in the West, and a host of new enterprises, it was clear that a new center of economic power was emerging in Canada west of Lake Superior. The talk in western Canada of separation from the East was now listened to more seriously. Like Quebec, western provinces demanded, in many cases, that the power concentrated in Ottawa should be decentralized to the provinces.

## 4. Canada in Crisis, 1975-79
### a. Foreign Investment

Concern about foreign investment was reflected in changes in the Income Tax Act in 1975, which cancelled a provision that allowed Canadian corporations to deduct advertising expenses in foreign-controlled publications, such as Time and Reader's Digest, from their taxes. Unless a magazine was 75 per cent Canadian owned and was noticeably different from its American counterpart, such deductions would not be allowed. Because advertising is the major prop of magazines such as this, the result was that the Canadian edition of *Time* was closed, while *Reader's Digest* made changes to satisfy the new ruling.

Petro-Canada was established as a Canadian-owned, government-supported company to increase Canadian presence in the oil industry, dominated almost totally by American-owned oil companies. But foreign investment was needed for Syncrude, a consortium of four American oil companies, combined with the Alberta and Canadian governments, to develop the Athabaska Tar Sands. In 1975, Atlantic Richfield withdrew, and the remaining American companies asked for changes in the agreement in order to continue in the project. Alberta took on additional expenditures in the project, totalling as much as $500 million, while Ottawa made a series of changes that allowed the participating companies to write off much of their development costs on their tax returns. The result, some critics suggested, was that the three remaining oil companies would pay 25 per cent of the costs of the Syncrude development while gaining a 70 per cent share ownership, while the Canadian and Alberta governments met 75 per cent of the costs, and gained a 30 per cent share of ownership.

### b. Native Peoples and Berger

For some generations, the population of Canada's native peoples had been on the rise, and it had become more politically active. At the same time, resource development sometimes disrupted native communities, whether it was a dam in Manitoba flooding native lands, a vast project such as the Quebec James Bay development that would transform their lands, or mercury pollution in northern Ontario that destroyed one of the major sources of food for a native community. In the Mackenzie Valley Pipeline project, the needs of southern communities for oil seemed to threaten the lifestyle of northern natives. After a series of meetings with native peoples in the Northwest Territories, Justice Tom Berger in 1977 recommended that the development be stopped. For perhaps the first time in Canadian history, a resource development had been halted because it was thought to do more harm than good. Northern communities that had counted on such resource development did not agree with the decision.

## c. Federal-Provincial Confrontations

In 1960, Quebec Premier, Jean Lesage, revived the idea of meetings between provincial premiers to discuss common problems with Ottawa. By the 1970's, such meetings had expanded dramatically in scope and frequency. Not only were the premiers meeting with each other, but their finance ministers, and their communications ministers, and a host of other officials were consulting together, with the federal government, on a wide range of topics. It seemed that such gatherings had become a permanent part of the Canadian scene.

Confrontations between Ottawa and the provinces developed on a great range of issues: communications, the financing of social benefits, oil resources, the constitution, offshore mineral rights. The most serious, perhaps, developed when Trudeau threatened to take action alone to bring the constitution back to Canada. Backed by most of the provinces, Bourassa said that such action would undermine the whole political structure of Canada. Trudeau's threat was not carried out.

## d. Wage and Price Controls

The Canadian economy continued to go sour. By 1975, unemployment had risen to 7 per cent of the labor force, while the rate of inflation per year had risen about 10 per cent. Canada had the worst strike record among developed countries in the world, with more hours lost due to industrial disputes, per capita, than anywhere else. While the total number of people employed had actually risen by 1.8 per cent over the year, unemployment still rose faster, because new workers came on the job market faster than the economy could absorb them.

In 1975, the federal government imposed wage and price controls. Both income and prices, said Trudeau, were rising faster than the value of the economy. A ceiling of 10 per cent was set on wage increases for 1975, to be followed by a ceiling of 8 per cent in 1976, and 6 per cent in 1977. Prices were to be held down, rising no faster than the increase in costs of materials and labor. An Anti-Inflation Review Board, and a Prices Review Board, were set up, with power to roll back wages and prices above the set limits. As it turned out, wages were held down, while prices, notably on food, were not.

The success of the program was disputed, but the effect for the Liberal party, it seemed, was a considerable loss of support among labor and consumers in general. It was widely felt that the government had to bear the responsibility for not having instituted a comprehensive economic plan. To many, the abruptly imposed set of controls was no substitute for such a plan. The controls eventually came to an end in the fall of 1978.

### e. Language

It was language, however, that became the most wrenching issue of the late 1970's. Quebec, the most bilingual province in Canada, was becoming more unilingual, just at the time when the federal government was promoting bilingualism in the rest of the country. Many observers suggested that, in fact, each area of the country was moving closer to a common practice in language policy. Nonetheless, the obvious contradiction in policies created massive tensions.

In 1974, Bill 22 was introduced in Quebec by the Bourassa government. It required that French be the language of normal communication in public administration, and, increasingly, in business. But it was the educational provisions that caused great controversy. While children of English-speaking parents would be taught in English, children whose parents were of a native tongue that was not English were required to attend French-language schools. The measure was attacked almost at once.

In the meantime, the federal bilingualism program was meeting increasing resistance. Language training programs seemed to make less impact and create more tensions, than they might have. Among federal civil servants, Anglophones generally failed to gain sufficient skill in the use of French. The result was often that, if a job required proficiency in both English and French, Francophones were more frequently successful in filling the requirements. Many anglophone civil servants, therefore, felt that their career advancement was threatened.

This issue exploded in 1976, in a dispute over air traffic control. As part of its bilingualism program, the federal government was gradually introducing bilingualism in air traffic control over selected airports in Quebec. Saying that they feared that this would endanger air safety, air traffic controllers and pilots went on strike, refusing to accept the bilingual policy of the federal government. Some of them, at least, seemed to feel that their advancement was threatened.

Almost without exception, English-speaking people throughout Canada supported them, and demanded a change in government policy. At the same time, French-speaking Canadians stood solidly behind French-speaking pilots and controllers, who disputed the claim that air safety was a valid issue. The government agreed to stop the introduction of bilingualism in air control until a commission, over which the controllers and pilots were given an effective veto, decided that no danger to safety existed.

Four months later, an election was held in Quebec. Bourassa had become personally unpopular in the province. His economic measures, including the vast James Bay project, had failed to reduce unemployment and alleviate poverty. Scandals had rocked his ministry, and local issues, such as federal milk pricing policies, had alienated voters. But the attack on bilingualism during the air control dispute had angered French-speaking Quebec. English Canada, it seemed to them, had rejected bilingualism, and the Trudeau government had given in to their pressure.

The Parti Quebecois gained 41.4 per cent of the popular vote, and 71 seats in the Quebec legislature. The Liberals won only 26 seats, on 33.8 per cent of the popular vote. The vote was not, many analysts suggested, a vote in favor of separation, but a vote in favor of good government. But the fact was that a party dedicated to separation had become the government of Quebec.

In 1977, the PQ introduced Bill 101, a far more stringent language bill than Bill 22. It was clearly aimed at making Quebec unilingual. Provisions requiring head offices to become more French-speaking helped to drive out the head office of Sun Life, the largest insurance company in the province. A significant number of anglophones moved from Montreal to other parts of Canada, and language disputes continued in the province. In 1978, French-language requirements for head offices were softened.

It was clear, in 1978, however, that Canada was facing the most serious crisis of its history. A referendum on separation was being organized by the PQ, and the future seemed uncertain.

## XXIV. The Turbulent Years 1979-1985

In the federal election held on May 22, 1979, the Conservatives returned to power under the leadership of Joe Clark. Clark, at 39, became Canada's youngest prime minister ever and the first Tory to serve in that capacity since John Diefenbaker sixteen years earlier. The Conservatives won 136 seats to the Liberal's 114 in the newly enlarged 282-seat House of Commons, even though the Liberals outpolled the Tories by four per cent in the popular vote. Thus, Canada was once more headed by a minority government.

The Liberal defeat reflected directly on Pierre Elliot Trudeau, coming after an election campaign that stressed leadership, to the exclusion of almost every other issue. During the campaign the Liberal strategy had been to depict Trudeau as the only leader with enough ability and experience to turn the economy around, maintain the authority of the central government and keep Quebec from breaking away. However, public uncertainty over Clark was not as strong as the voters' concern over economic issues. Under Trudeau, Canada's economy had been perplexingly stagnant for a nation so rich in resources: its unemployment rate had been hovering around 9 per cent and its inflation rate was just under 10 per cent at the time the election was called. Furthermore, the weakening of the Canadian dollar had dramatically raised the cost of imports and of travel abroad. After eleven years of flamboyant and often controversial leadership, Trudeau had worn out his welcome with many voters.

Joe Clark, meanwhile, had run a cautious, controlled campaign. He repeatedly promised to cut taxes, curb inflation and reduce unemployment. Of all his campaign promises the most popular one by far dealt with the provision of tax deductions for home mortgage interest payments and home property tax.

Soon after the election Clark learned how hard it would be to carry out all the planks of his party's campaign platform. His promise to move the Canadian embassy in Israel, from Tel Aviv to Jerusalem, had to be abandoned in light of Arab economic pressure. Also, his proposal to sell Petro-Canada to private investors, thus allowing the National Energy Board to buy all foreign oil, and letting private oil companies carry out all frontier exploration, came under heavy fire. The opposition parties threatened to unite to bring down the Conservative government if Clark attempted to implement this policy.

During the first week of the new Parliament in October, Clark was defending the third Bank of Canada rate hike since becoming Prime Minister. The rate increases in Canada and the United States were jolting an already overpriced market. Stocks faltered while consumers and borrowers shouldered the news that loan rates were moving still higher. Angry MP's demanded an explanation.

Before Christmas Trudeau announced he would resign as Liberal leader, and an election was in the offing.

The Clark government's first budget included a boost in oil prices and new taxes on gasoline, tobacco and alchohol. This all threatened a new round of inflation. The Finance Minister, John Crosbie, pledged it would mean a reduced deficit and better future growth.

With this budget the Clark government would fall. He'd been Prime Minister for only 206 days. The Conservatives had miscalculated the Liberals' mood following Trudeau's announced resignation. The Tories expected they would get the budget through while the Liberals searched for a new leader. But by week's end Trudeau said he might stay on.

The Conservative government was defeated in a non-confidence motion. In the election campaign that followed, the sole issue was energy prices. Clark's proposal for new or increased taxes on fuel had farmers and fishermen furious. On February 18, the Trudeau Liberals won 146 seats, a parliamentary majority, the Tories only 103, the NDP 32.

## Referendum 1980

In early November, 1979, the Quebec government published a White Paper on the referendum, outlining its proposal for "sovereignty-association." The paper played on Quebeckers' fears for their future as a separate minority within Canada.

But they also feared for their economic security. Within minutes of the polls closing on May 20, the results were clear. 59% of Quebec voters had rejected "sovereignty-association."

## The Constitution Act — 1982

In 1980 Canada's constitution was a combination of the 1867 British North America Act, certain statutes of Parliament, and unwritten traditions. But it did not define which level of government was responsible for many issues, nor did it offer human rights guarantees.

The constitution was one of Trudeau's priorities — he wanted to bring it home. But changes in the distribution of power could only be done with the consent of all 11 governments. It was back to the bargaining table in November and an agreement was reached. On December 2, the Commons voted 246 to 24 to approve the resolution to bring the constitution home. On April 17, 1982, the Queen and the Prime Minister signed the proclamation. The Constitution Act of 1982 replaced the BNA Act of 1867.

For the first time Canadians had a constitution that was legal in both languages. It included a charter of fundamental rights and a formula for future amendments. It guaranteed that both English and French could be used in Parliament, federal courts, and any federal government office. Where numbers warranted, Francophones would have the right to educate their children in French schools. There was a charter that entrenched basic freedoms and legal and equality rights. Those freedoms embraced religion, the press, and peaceful assembly; the right to call a lawyer "without delay" and not to be detained arbitrarily; freedom of equal treatment regardless of race, origin, color, religion, sex, age, or disability.

Alteration of the Senate or Supreme Court had to be approved by seven provinces represented 50% of the population. Ontario and Quebec no longer had a veto.

## 1981 and 1982

In 1981 inflation soared to its highest level since the 1930s. The dollar fell to an all-time low. Interest rates climbed to 23%. Ottawa and Edmonton hammered out a new $212 billion energy agreement. Ottawa intervened with oil and gas firms as companies were "Canadianized."

Trudeau was expected to resign that year but decided not to.

Unemployment created a horde of jobless. While protests and strikes grew commonplace, men and women who took part in demonstrations eyed their own leaders with wariness.

North America during 1981 had moved into the worst recession since the 1930s. Losses on the Toronto Stock Exchange amounted to more than $20 billion. Businesses across the country were going bankrupt at the rate of 2,500 each month.

The Bank of Canada's monetary policy was most to blame because it raised interest rates to an unprecedented 23%.

1982 was a year of misfortune everywhere in the country. Bankruptcies rose by 35%. The collapse of Dome Petroleum, a major oil company, was averted by a $1 billion bail-out.

The government offered few solutions to the crisis other than a "Six-and-Five" wage restraint program and ill-defined job programs.

On the positive side, interest rates dropped to 15%, inflation subsided, and the constitution finally came home.

The Liberals' popularity plummeted while a Conservative trend emerged from that year's provincial elections. Despite the polls, Joe Clark could not quell the mutinous factions within his own party. And Trudeau showed no signs of resigning.

## 1983

On January 28, Conservative delegates voted on the subject of a leadership review. Clark won the support of only 69.9% of the delegates. Amid a chorus of "No, no, no," Clark recommended to the party executive that a leadership convention be called.

At that convention, on the fourth ballot, it was a two-way fight between Clark and Mulroney. Mulroney won the race, 1,584 votes to 1,325.

By year's end, the economy looked brighter. On January 6, for the first time in four years, the Bank of Canada rate dropped below 10%. By the end of the year, corporate profits were running 45% ahead of 1982, and the next capital spending boom had begun.

## 1984

1984 saw a withering of Canadian nationalism. Citizens were calling for foreign investment to help create jobs.

In Quebec, the nationalist ferment was over. The Parti-Quebecois seemed to have no future and the Union Nationale was bouncing back.

Pierre Trudeau resigned on February 29. After 15 years he was gone, not very different from the mysterious stranger he was when Canadians welcomed him in 1968.

Fifteen weeks later the Liberals held a leadership convention. In the end John Turner won over Jean Chretien, 1,862 to 1,368.

Turner made a serious mistake in calling a snap election. It caught his party unprepared, while the Tories had been ready for a year. And Turner's decision to announce Trudeau's appointments of 17 MP's to patronage jobs the day before he called the election added fuel to Mulroney's campaign.

On September 4, the Conservatives won in a landslide. Canada elected 211 Tories, only 40 Liberals, and 30 NDPs.

Mulroney's victory brought with it hope and expectations. The nation's 1.3 million unemployed will expect the new Tory government to create jobs but the business community will look for measures to trim the deficit and improve the investment climate. The provinces will expect a co-operative era in federal-provincial relations. And all Canadians will be looking for signs that official co-operation will pay dividends in daily life.

# Bibliography

Berger, Carl. *Imperialism and Nationalism, 1884-1914: A Conflict in Canadian Thought,* Toronto: Copp Clark Pub. Co., 1969.

Bliss, Michael. *A Living Profit,* Toronto: McClelland and Stewart Ltd., 1974.

Brown, R.C., and Ramsay Cook. *Canada 1896-1921: A Nation Transformed,* Toronto: McClelland and Stewart Ltd., 1976.

Bumsted, J.M., ed. *Documentary Problems in Canadian History: Pre-Confederation,* Vol. I, Georgetown, Ont.: Irwin-Dorsey Ltd., 1969.

Careless, J.M.S., ed. *Colonists and Canadians 1760-1867,* Toronto: Macmillan of Canada, 1971.

Careless, J.M.S., and R.C. Brown. *The Canadians 1867-1967* Toronto: Macmillan of Canada, 1976.

Clark, S.D., J.P. Grayson and L.M. Grayson, eds. *Prophecy and Protest,* Toronto: Gage Educational Pub. Ltd., 1975.

Cook, Ramsay, Craig Brown and Carl Berger, eds. *Approaches to Canadian History,* Toronto: University of Toronto Press, 1974.

Cook, Ramsay, Craig Brown and Carl Berger. *Imperial Relations in the Age of Laurier,* Toronto: University of Toronto Press, 1969.

Copp, Terry. *The Anatomy of Poverty,* Toronto: McClelland and Stewart Ltd., 1974.

Creighton, Donald. *The Forked Road Canada 1939-1957,* Toronto: McClelland and Stewart Ltd., 1976.

Creighton, Donald. *The Story of Canada,* Toronto: Macmillan of Canada, 1971.

Dunham, Aileen. *Political Unrest in Canada 1815-1836,* Toronto: McClelland and Stewart Ltd., 1963.

Fraser, Blair. *The Search for Identity in Canada: Post War to Present,* Toronto: Doubleday Canada Ltd., 1967.

Horn, Michael, and Ronald Sabourin. *Canadian Social History,* Toronto: McClelland and Stewart Ltd., 1974.

Lower, J.A. *Canada An Outline History,* Toronto: McGraw-Hill Ryerson Ltd., 1973.

Maclean's Magazine, Weekly Issues 1979-1985

Morton, W.L. *The Canadian Identity,* Toronto: University of Toronto Press, 1972.

Perkins, Bradford. *The Causes of the War of 1812,* Huntington, N.Y.: Robert E. Krieger Pub. Co., 1978.

Stursberg, Peter. *Diefenbaker Leadership Gained, 1956-62,* Toronto: University of Toronto Press, 1975.